FIELD GUIDE
TO
REVENUE STAMPED PAPER

Being a
Priced Catalog of Civil War and Spanish American
War Checks, Drafts, Receipts, Stocks, Bonds, and
other Documents Bearing Imprinted Revenue Stamps

Part 1

THE WESTERN STATES

Arizona, California, Colorado,
Hawaii, Idaho, Montana, Nevada,
New Mexico, Oregon, Utah,
Washington, Wyoming,
British Columbia and *Chihuahua*

compiled by B.J. Castenholz

Castenholz and Sons
Publishers
1055 Hartzell Street
Pacific Palisades, California 90272

This Work is Dedicated
to the Memory of
J. Paul Castenholz
1904 — 1988
He gave me a full measure
of his own enjoyment in philately.

CONTENTS

FOREWARD

If you collect or study the United States imprinted revenue documents, you are venturing into the most fertile of all philatelic adventures. Imprinted revenue paper has it all: there are a great variety of stamp designs, most of them very beautiful; the stamps were printed in almost endless colors and shades; and many spectacular printing errors occur.

Many imprint types and varieties are rare — it is not unusual to find major pieces with a total census of less than 5 to 10 known. And discoveries are still being made: perhaps 15 varieties or more have come to light just since 1980, including a number of inverts, new type/color combinations, a new major variety for Nevada, and a number of restrictive clause varieties.

Within the last 20 years there have been such discoveries as the S-type without restrictive clause (of which now perhaps 11 are known from 2 different users!) and a Type T with restrictive clause as occurs on T8, but in type rather than within a tablet. This latter variety is only known by 2 cut squares.

Many collectors have held cut squares in low esteem until they found certain varieties (such as R7, T7, and several varieties of Type U) to be virtually unattainable except in cut form.

Leaving the stamp varieties for a moment, the challange of collecting imprinted revenue paper by type of document is another nearly endless pursuit. In addition to checks, drafts and receipts from fabulous places of the past such as Virginia City in Nevada, Bodie in California and Kit Carson in Colorado there are signatures from the famous and not-so-famous. Great corporations and great manipulators of fortunes are represented. The growth of the railroads is well illustrated in the stocks and bonds from the great roads that spanned the continent to the short lines that later became parts of the few railroads that survived into the 20th century. The banknote companies produced some spectacularly beautiful checks, drafts and receipts as well as the larger certificates, the stocks, bonds, and insurance policies.

A study of the proliferation of imprinted revenue paper gives a good deal of insight into the commerce of the day. Here a comparison of the population of imprinted documents from one part of the country to another, or from a particular place in the Post-Bellum Period (1865-1883) to that distribution of users at the turn of the century (the Spanish American War imprinted paper being used from 1898 to 1902) gives growth patterns of unusual interest. For example, there are far more California users of the Type X than for the Civil War issues. But in Nevada the opposite is true: Nevada users of the time following the Civil War are far more plentiful than the pieces of the turn of the century (undoubtedly due to the depletion of silver in the Comstock).

OVERALL PLAN OF THE FIELD GUIDE

The intent of this work is to publish, in approximately seven parts, all known United States imprinted revenue documents, listed by users. Most parts will be geographically arranged. However, it is expected that at least one part will be devoted to the larger documents — stocks, bonds, insurance policies, etc. As the larger documents will be covered in the geographical parts as well, some overlapping of listings would occur.

The first edition of each part will be a trial list. As such completeness can not be expected. Later editions will be as complete as possible. An example of this occurs here in Part 1. The Nevada trial list was first published in *The American Revenuer,* April, 1986. It included 97 entries. The Nevada listing presented here includes over 150 entries. And although it appears that the list is approaching completeness, pleasant surprises are still very likely.

There are several pieces, the existance of which is not in doubt but which are not listed here. Some of them have not been seen by this compiler, which in most cases leaves doubt as to the imprint color, check colors, paper color or printer. One or two pieces have been seen but no photographic or xerographic record could be made. They also have been omitted.

PRICING

The valuations in this catalog have been made on the basis of rarity and collectability: a combination of general appearance, quality of production, type of document, how well known or important the user is, the place of use, and any other historical significance. Of course auction records and current market conditions are strong factors in pricing.

While condition is often the dominent factor in much of philately, a more reasonable attitude exists in the revenue stamped paper field. If the imprint is rare, the condition is important. But for the more common imprints a clean document with some enhancement, such as a beautiful vignette or an important source, can have a good market value even with a punch hole in the imprint.

A WORD OF CAUTION

Revenue stamped paper finds occur frequently. It will not be unusual, especially in this awakening period when so much new interest is developing, to find pieces not listed in this catalog. Many pieces listed here and priced modestly, are quite scarce. New finds must be taken in that light, and not assumed to be extremely valuable just because the pieces are not listed in this trial list. Common sense should prevail.

IMPRINT COLORS

The imprint colors have been fairly well established by Scott in their *Specialized Catalogue of United States Stamps.* Only a few deviations from that catalogue have been made here, namely the color yellow is not used in this catalog, and D3 (brown) has been included in the D1 listings.

Because of the extent of the variations in the color orange, and the absence of an imprint in true yellow (with no trace of red), no yellow listings have been included. In every case where a 'yellow' has been seen, it has proved to contain some red.

A true brown has not been seen for D3. The buff is indeed a good color, in many cases distinct from orange. But the nearly continual color gradations that exists between orange and buff are such that it is a matter of choice as to where the division occurs between the two colors. The issue has simply been sidestepped, and all of the buffs have been included in the oranges of D1.

Violet is used when red dominates, purple is used when blue is dominant.

A personal observation: I have never seen a red Type C, all are pink; except for proofs, every Type W piece listed as brown has so far turned out to be brownish orange.

ABBREVIATIONS

All state abbreviations used here are according to *current* Post Office Department designations. Names of major cities are not usually followed by their state designations, unless confusion would result.

HOW TO USE THE CATALOG

The catalog portion of this work is organized in such a way as to incorporate the most possible information in the most concise manner.

A typical entry looks like this:

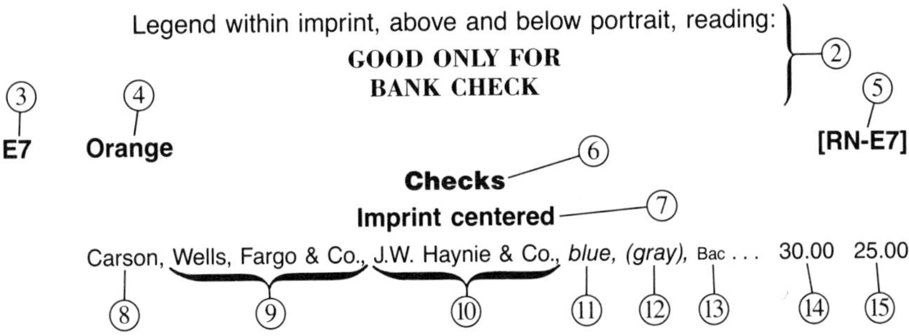

1. Designation of the major imprint die classification as set down by Vanderhoof.
2. Specific description of the imprint legend, if present. The legend is shown *exactly* as it reads, including style of typeface used.
3. The catalog number of the imprint type as used in this work. It is, with a few exceptions, the same as the Scott Catalog Number (except, of course Scott numbers always use the prefix RN-).
4. Basic color of the imprint and legend, if present. See comments on colors.
5. Scott Catalog Number, as used in the Scott's *1988 Specialized Catalog of United States Stamps.*
6. Type of document.
7. Position of imprint on document. When given as centered, it is approximate.
8. City, town, or specific location as noted on the document. Normally printed, but occasionally manuscript (ms).

    –, indicates same location as preceeding entry.

    –, –, indicates all information is as the preceeding entry, except as indicated.

    ▲ indicates "STAMP REDEEMED" reading up.
    ▼ indicates "STAMP REDEEMED" reading down.
    ▶ indicates "STAMP REDEEMED" reading horizontal.

9. Issuing agency, normally a financial institution. In the case of a draft, the firm drawn upon is not normally noted.
10. Individual account involved.
    ✂ indicates document not complete. Normally this involves the removal of the individual account name at the extreme left end of the document.
11. Color used to print the document (not the imprint). If simply black on white, no colors are noted. Handstamp and manuscript (ms) colors are given where used for significant elements of the document, such as bank or account names, 'GOLD,' 'SILVER,' 'ORIGINAL,' etc. Colors of numbers are not included.
12. Paper color. This, generally would be the color of the back of the document if the face is printed all-over.
13. A three letter designation of the printer of the document (not the imprint). The list of printers and their designations follows the catalog listings.
14. A price in this column indicates the value of an unused example. No price indicates an unused example has not been seen by this cataloguer.
15. A price in this column indicates the value of a used example. No price indicates a used example has not been seen by this cataloguer.

REFERENCES TO SCOTT'S CATALOG

All references made in this catalog to Scott's Catalog or Scott's Catalog Numbers refer to Scott's *1988 Specialized Catalogue of United States Stamps,* copyright 1987 Amos Philatelics, Inc., dba Scott Publishing Co.

THANKS

I must thank Ken Harrison, Eric Jackson and Charles Kemp for their contributions to the pricing. However, the final responsibility is mine.

And I want to express my appreciation for all those who have generously provided information and particulars on various revenue stamped paper documents. It has been a practice, however, that all pieces catalogued here have been seen by me.

METHODS OF PRINTING

There were three possible methods used to print the stamps: letterpress, engraving and lithography. First, a brief review of the different processes. Letterpress printing uses metal or wood type and clichés or stereotypes. The high surfaces are inked and pressed against the surface of the paper, producing the desired image. Engraving forms an image from recesses cut into a smooth plate. Ink is applied to the plate, wiped from the smooth surface, remaining only in the recesses. Paper, usually dampened to increase its ability to conform to small irregularities, is then pressed against the surface of the plate, conforming slightly to the recesses, where the ink is contacted by the paper, thus producing the image. Lithography prints from a flat surface, part of which has been sensitized, usually photographically, to hold ink, which is an oil based substance. The non-sensitized portion of the surface is wetted with a water solution, and the ink adheres only where the surface is not wetted. The entire plate contacts the paper but only the sensitized areas bearing the ink print the image.

Interestingly, each printing process leaves its own characteristics on the printed work. Letterpress work most often shows an impression on the back of the printed paper. And, often the impression shows the edge of the type or cliché on the face side. Engraving uses a type of ink which stands above the surface of the paper, giving a slightly raised feel. Most often, the reverse shows slight hollows where the paper has been pressed into the tiny recesses in the engraved plate. Lithography has none of the characteristics of either letterpress work or engraving. The edges of the type and design are not usually quite as sharp as the other two methods, and often minor dots and blemishes appear in the fields.

Butler and Carpenter produced imprint Types H, I and J by engraving. Scott's *Specialized Catalogue of United States Stamps,* states that the imprints were lithographed, with the exception of Types H, I and J. (Apparently Butler and Carpenter also produced Type K, but not by engraving.) The balance of the revenue imprints were produced by *letterpress* printing! Although it is not possible to say with certainty that lithography was never used, the evidence strongly suggests that it was not.

THE PRINTERS

The United States revenue stamped paper is very unusual in many respects. From a philatelic point of view, not much fundamental research has been done, with the result that several elementary questions remain unanswered. Were the stamps printed entirely by the firms that developed the various designs? What were the purposes of the restrictive clauses? Was there any relationship between the printers of the stamps and the printers of the documents? Which were printed first, the documents or the imprints? Was that order of printing always consistant? Did the color of the imprint have any significance?

To provide information that might lead to some of the answers to the above questions, the listings in this catalog include the printer of the document, whenever that information is available. The **List of Printers** gives the names of the printers and the corresponding three-letter designations used in the catalog. The list includes all printers that have been seen on revenue stamped paper of both the Civil War and the Spanish-American War periods. Many of the printers on the list are not represented by documents from the Western States.

NUMBERING SYSTEM

A system for numbering every piece listed in this catalog was given a great deal of consideration. The concept was rejected because entries added to a revised edition would render the numbers used in this edition obsolete. And great confusion could occur in auction and dealer offerings as well. It is planned to employ numbering in a later edition.

Arizona

Type G

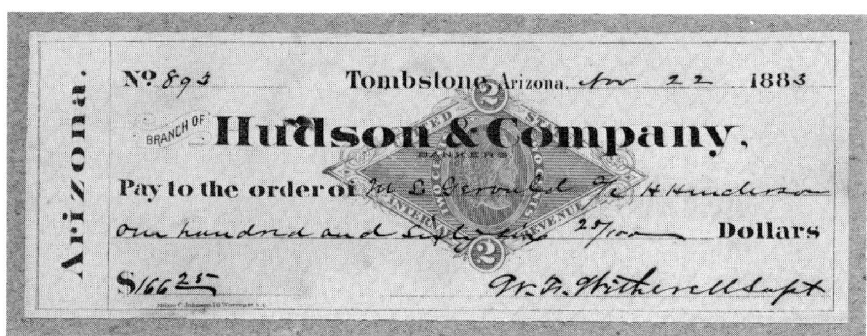

G1   Orange   **[RN-G1]**

Checks
Imprint centered

Tombstone, Cochise County Bank, (two settings), WmM	15.00	15.00
—, Hudson & Co, Bankers, *black, blue tint*, MCJ		15.00
—, Agency Pima County Bk, WmM		15.00

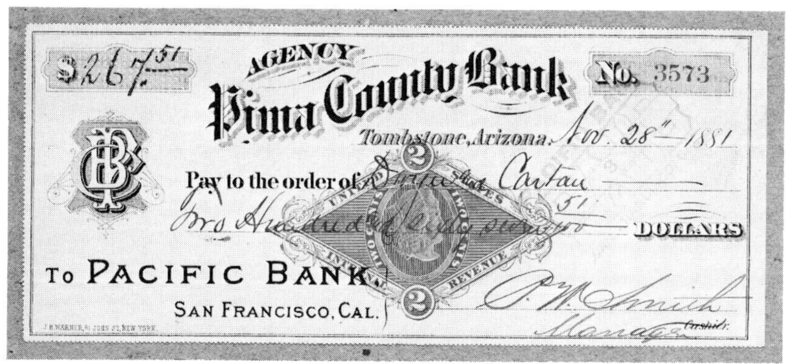

Drafts
Imprint centered

Tombstone, Cochise County Bk, Ban	25.00
—, Agency Pima County Bk, *(pink)*, JHW	25.00
—, —, *(yellow)*, JHW	25.00
—, —, *(green)*, JHW	25.00
Tucson, Pima County Bk, *(yellow)*, WmM	25.00

Type X

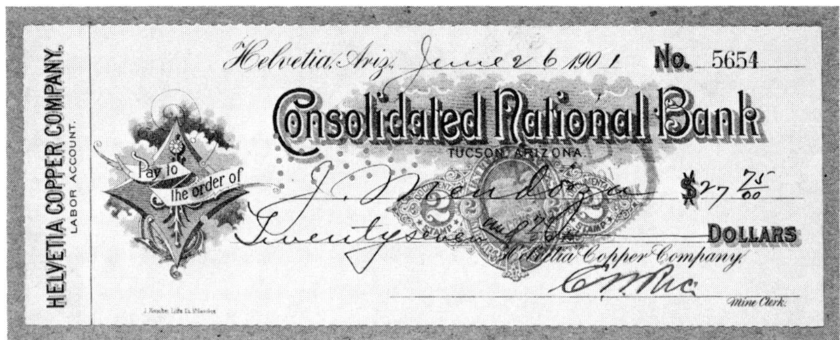

X7   Orange   **[RN-X7]**

Checks

Imprint centered

Helvetia, Consolidated Nat Bk,
    Helvetia Copper Co., *black, red,* K&C 18.00
Phoenix, Valley Bk, *(cream),* Hal 9.00
Prescott, Bk of Arizona 9.00
—, Prescott Nat Bk, Santa Fe, Prescott & Phoenix Railway Co.,
    black, pink tint, Hal 12.00
—, —, Castle Creek Hot Springs & Improvement Co., *black, violet,* Hal   12.00

Type B

B1 **Orange** [RN-B1]

Checks
Imprint centered

San Francisco, London and San Francisco Bk, *red,* H&C 5.00 5.00
—, —, *blue,* LeC 5.00
—, Agency First Nat Bk of Nevada, *red,* WHA 10.00
—, John Sime & Co. Bankers, MSC 9.00

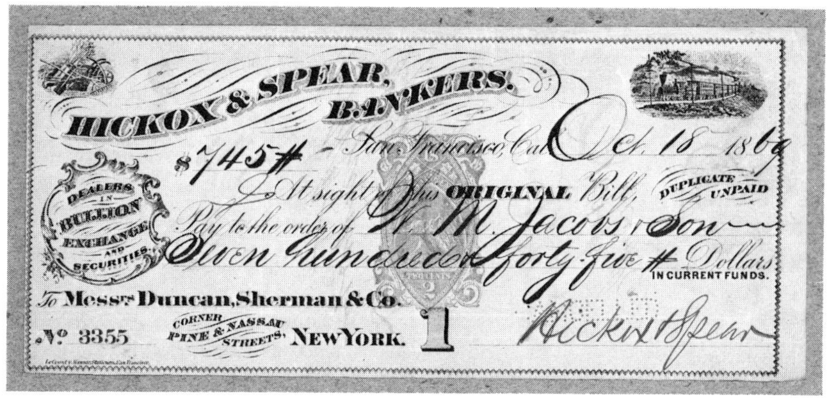

Bills of Exchange
Imprint centered

San Francisco, Hickox & Spear, *red, black,* LeC 20.00

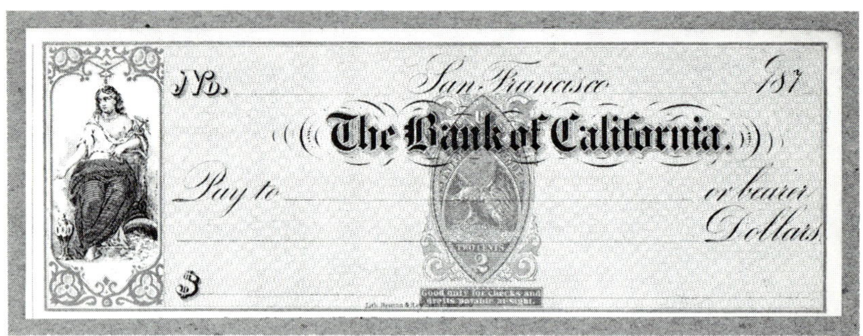

Rectangular tablet below imprint, reading:

**Good only for checks and
drafts payable at sight.**

B16   Orange   [RN-B16]

Checks

Imprint centered

San Francisco, Bk of California, *brown, yellow, yellow tint,* B&R 65.00
—, —, North Pacific Transportation Co., B&R 7.50
—, Tallant & Co., Bankers, *brown,* B&R 20.00

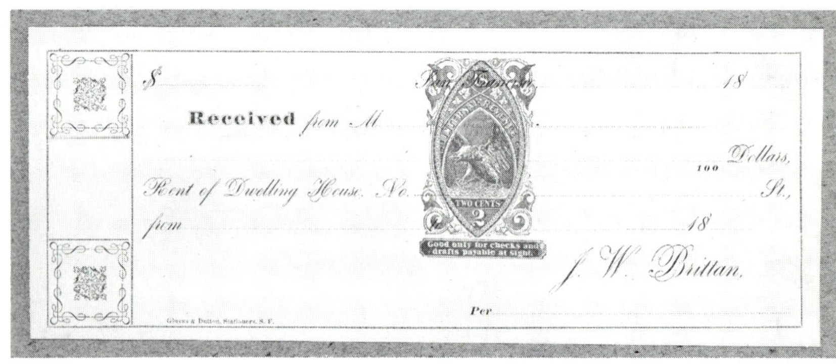

Octagonal tablet below imprint, reading:

**Good only for checks and
drafts payable at sight.**

B17   Orange   [RN-B17]

Checks

Imprint centered

San Francisco, Bk of California, North Pacific Transportation Co., B&R   7.50
—, —, same, w/Vitale ad on back 7.50
—, Donohoe, Kelly & Co., Bankers, EBC 22.50
—, Parrott & Co., Bankers, Bac 8.00
—, Tallant & Co., Bankers, *brown* 25.00

Receipts (improper use)
Imprint centered
Check size

San Francisco, J.W. Brittan, G&P 75.00

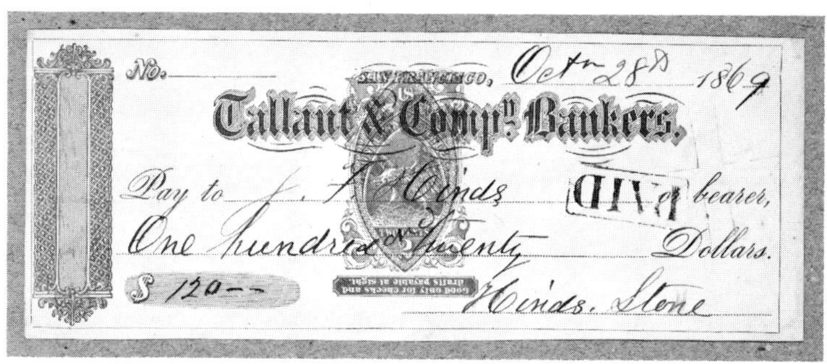

As last type, but with octagonal tablet inverted

B17a Orange [RN-B17a]

Checks
Imprint centered

San Francisco, Tallant & Co., Bankers, *brown* 750.00

Typeset legend below imprint, reading:
**Good when issued for the
payment of money.**

B23 Orange [RN-B23]

Receipts
Imprint centered

San Francisco, Richard Patrick & Co., *violet,* G&G 500.00

Type C

C1   Orange   [RN-C1]

Checks
Imprint centered

San Francisco, Pacific Bk, LeC 25.00

Bills of Exchange
Imprint centered

Sacramento, Nat Gold Bk of D.O. Mills & Co., *black, red HS,* ABN ..   80.00

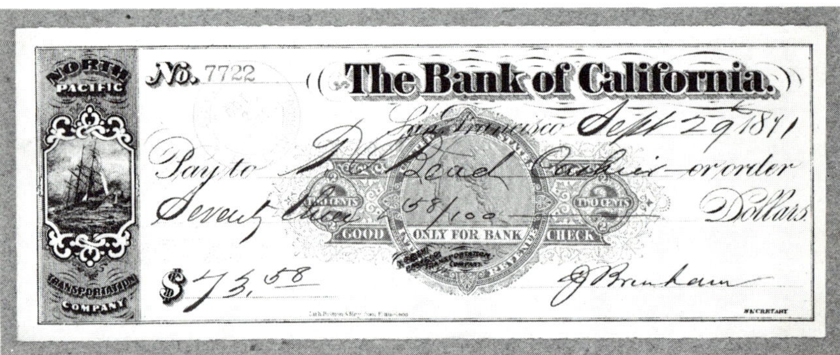

Three part band across lower half of imprint, reading:

GOOD   **ONLY FOR BANK**   **CHECK**

C21   Orange   [RN-C21]

Checks
Imprint centered

Los Angeles, Caswell & Ellis, ALB 20.00
San Francisco, Bk of California 10.00
—, —, *brown, yellow, yellow tint,* B&R 60.00

—, —, City Paving Co., *blue,* JGH 15.00
—, —, La Grange Ditch and Hydraulic Mining Co., ... 18.00
—, —, North Pacific Transportation Co., B&R 9.00
—. —, same, w/Vitale ad on back 10.00
—, Belloc Freres, Frank G. Edwards, *red,* EBC 18.00
—, California Trust Co., GTB 12.00
—, Donohoe, Kelly & Co., EBC 10.00
San Jose, McLaughlin & Ryland, San Jose Water Co., *violet* 15.00

C22   Brown   **[RN-C22]**

Checks
Imprint centered

San Francisco, Bk of California 25.00
—, North Pacific Transportation Co., B&R 22.50

Type D

D1   Orange   **[RN-D1]**

Checks
Imprint centered

Chico, Bk of Butte County, *violet,* Bac 20.00
Chinese Camp, London and San Francisco Bk, Ltd, Martin Bacon, *red* 30.00
Dixon, Bk of Dixon, *violet,* Fra 20.00
Healdsburg, Nat Gold Bk and Trust Co.,
      Canan, Hutton & Smith, Bankers, *blue,* W&C 20.00
Sacramento, Nat Gold Bk of D.O. Mills & Co., H&S................. 5.00
San Francisco, Bk of California 8.00
—, —, Pacific Mail Steam Ship Co., *brown* 20.00
—, Donohoe, Kelly & Co., F&V 6.00   5.00
—, First Nat Gold Bk, *black, pink tint,* Cro 5.00
—, London & San Francisco Bk, 'SILVER,' *blue*................. 10.00
—, —,*red,* C&S... 5.00
—, Merchants Exchange Bk, P.C. Dart........................... 5.00
—, Daniel Meyer, Gila Silver Mining Co., HaP 10.00
—, Nat Gold Bk and Trust Co., *red* 8.00
—, —, Cro 5.00
—, Pacific Bk, *black, red*................................... 25.00

—, Sather & Co., *violet,* Ste 5.00
—, —, EBC 6.00
—, —, *red,* BFS 6.00
—, Swiss American Bk, *violet,* EBC 8.00
—, Well, Fargo & Co. 10.00
San Luis Obispo, Bank of San Luis Obispo, JGH 12.00

Drafts
Imprint centered

Dixon, Bk of Dixon, *brown, purple HS, brown tint,* M&K 15.00
La Porte, Bk of La Porte, B&R 10.00
Los Angeles, Farmers and Merchants Bk of Los Angeles, B&R 18.00
San Francisco, Hickox & Spear, *black, brown tint,* WPH 10.00

Legend to left and right, within circles of imprint, reading:

GOOD   **BANK**
ONLY FOR   **CHECK**

D7   **Orange**   **[RN-D7]**

Checks
Imprint centered

Folsom, Wells, Fargo & Co., Alexander & Hyman, *red* 16.00
San Luis Obispo, Bk of San Luis Obispo, changed from
    Nat Gold Bk & Trust Co., San Francisco, (ms) *red,* W&C 12.00
San Francisco, Bk of California, *green, yellow tint.* 20.00
—, —, Cheesman, Head & Thornburgh, *black, red,* B&R 10.00
—, —, North Pacific Transportation Co., B&R 7.50
—, Tallant & Co., *green,* B&R 20.00

Drafts (improper use)
Imprint centered

Los Angeles, Caswell & Ellis, *blue*, ALB 20.00

Type E

Legend within imprint, above and below portrait, reading:

**GOOD ONLY FOR
BANK CHECK**

E7   Orange   **[RN-E7]**

Checks
Imprint centered

Goodyear's (ms changed from Marysville), Decker & Jewett, *violet,* Bac   25.00
La Porte, California Trust Co., Bk of La Porte, *red,* WNC 20.00
North Bloomfield, Gold Canon Mining Co.,
   (ms altered from Yuba Gravel Mining Co.), *blue, pink tint* 25.00
Oakland, Oakland Bk of Savings, EBC. 25.00
San Francisco, Belloc Freres, *red,* EBC. 40.00   20.00

Type F

F1   Orange   **[RN-F1]**

Checks
Imprint centered

Folsom, Wells, Fargo & Co., J. Hyman, *(brown)*		15.00
Sacramento, Odd Fellows' Savings and Commercial Bk, ✂, *(brown)*		8.00
San Francisco, Alfred Borel & Co., *violet, orange tint,* HaP	10.00	
—, Anglo Californian Bk, Fra	10.00	
—, Bk of California, B&R	10.00	
—, London & San Francisco Bk, *red,* C&S		8.00
—, Merchants Exchange Bk, 'GOLD,'		7.00
—, —, 'SILVER,' *blue*	7.00	
—, Nevada Bk of San Francisco, *brown,* B&R	8.00	6.00
—, —, W.S. Hobart, *brown, red,* B&R		6.00
—, Pacific Bk, *black, red HS*	6.00	
—, Pacific Exchange, *red*		7.00
—, Wells Fargo & Co's Bk		10.00

Drafts
Imprint centered

La Porte, Bk of La Porte, B&R	8.00

Bills of Exchange
Imprint centered

San Francisco, Bk of California, *red-brown,* ABN	25.00

Type G

G1   Orange   **[RN-G1]**

Checks
Imprint centered

Antioch (ms), Pacific Bank, *black, gray tint*	14.00
Bodie, Bodie Bk, bk name in outline italics	20.00
—, —, bk name in bold italics	20.00
—, —, EAC	20.00
Columbia, Wells Fargo & Co's Bk, H. Sevening, Bac	15.00
Chico, Bk of Butte County, *violet*	15.00
Grass Valley (ms), F. Berton & Co., *violet,* EBC	12.00
Los Angeles, Commercial Bk, *violet,* CAB	15.00

—, Farmers' and Merchants' Bk............................... 15.00
—, —, *blue*.. 15.00
Martinez (HS changed from San Francisco), Bk of California,
    Fish & Blum, *black, purple HS, pink tint,* B&R.............. 15.00
—, Bk of Martinez, Fish & Blum, Dor......................... 15.00
Red Bluff, Bk of Tehama County 12.00
Sacramento, California State Bk, *black, gray tint,* HSC ....◆ 8.00
—, Capitol Savings (ms changed from
    Odd Fellows' Savings and Commercial Bk), *(brown)*........... 6.00
—, (Sacramento in ms), Nat Gold Bk of D.O. Mills & Co., *(brown)*.. 8.00
—, —, *(brown),* Cro....................................... 8.00
—, —, *(brown),* WWG...................................... 8.00
—, —, bk name paste-up,
    N.L. Drew & Co. (lined out), *black, pink tint,* CBN, Cro........... 10.00
San Bernardino, Bk of San Bernardino, ALB 15.00
San Diego, Consolidated Bk of San Diego (HS changed
    from Commercial Bk of San Diego), *black, red HS,* CMC 15.00
—, —, Western Union Tel. Co., *black, violet, (brown),* A&B........ 25.00
—, Consolidated Bk, *black, gray tint,* CMC..................... 15.00
San Francisco, Anglo Californian Bk, *blue,* Fra................. 10.00
—, Bk of California, B&R.................................. 10.00
—, —, *(violet),* B&R 10.00
—, —, *red,* B&R 10.00
—, —, D.O. Mills monogram to left 10.00
—, —, Wason Con. Mng. Co., *red,* B&R 10.00
—, —, Coll Deane, *blue,* B&R 12.00
—, —, Estate of John G. Hodge & Co., *violet, (violet)*............ 10.00
—, —, Gen'l Lee S.M. Co's Office, LBr 15.00
—, Belloc & Cie., *blue* 8.00
—, Ir. Belloc, *light brown*................................. 8.00
—, B. Davidson & Co., B&R 15.00
—, Donohoe, Kelly & Co. 5.00
—, —, AJL... 5.00
—, —, same but frame line around check..................... 4.00
—, —, F&V... 5.00
—, —, CGC 5.00
—, —, *(violet),* F&V...................................... 5.00
—, —, *(violet),* CGC 5.00
—, First Nat Gold Bk, *black, pink tint,* Cro 10.00
—, —, 'GOLD,' ('SILVER' lined out), *black, red, pink tint,* Cro 10.00
—, —, Bay Sugar Refinery, FLF 12.00
—, —, Seal Rock Tobacco Co., HSC 15.00
—, Lazard Frères, PUC.................................... 6.00
—, —, B&R 8.00 6.00
—, —, *black, violet tint,* B&R 8.00
—, —, *(brown)*... 7.00
—, —, bk name paste-up over Bk of California, B&R 6.00
—, —, bk name paste-up over Wells Fargo & Co's Bk, B&R........ 6.00
—, London & San Francisco Bk, *red,* LBr.............. 10.00 5.00
—, —, *red,* C&S 10.00 5.00
—, Nevada Bk of San Francisco, *brown,* B&R 10.00
—, —, W.S. Hobart, *brown,* B&R 9.00
—, Pacific Bk, *(brown),* B&R................................ 9.00

—, Sather & Co., *brown,* Ste 6.00
—, —, California Iron & Steel Co., BEP 15.00
—, Tallant & Co., *brown,* B&R 12.00
—, Wells Fargo & Co's Bk 10.00
—, —, J.P. Jones, B&R 12.00
San Jose, Commercial and Savings Bk, MCJ 10.00
—, First Nat Bk 10.00
San Luis Obispo, Bk of San Luis Obispo, JGH 10.00
—, —, CCW 10.00
Santa Rosa, Santa Rosa Bk 16.00
—, Savings Bk of Santa Rosa 16.00
Sawyer's Bar, Cross & Co., Black Bear Quartz Mg. Co., B&R 25.00

Drafts
Imprint centered

Bodie, Bodie Bk, bk name in shaded caps, *black, pink tint* 50.00
—, —, Outline 'B's in bk name, *black, gray tint, (blue)* 50.00
Dixon, Bk of Dixon, 'SILVER' lined out, *brown, purple HS,* ALB 15.00
La Porte, Bk of La Porte, B&R 13.00

Type X

X7   Orange   **[RN-X7]**

Checks
Imprint centered

Auburn, Placer County Bk,
    Jupiter Consolidated Gravel Mining Co., *black, violet HS,* ULC . . .   10.00
Bakersfield, Kern Valley Bk, El Dorado Oil Co., *black, purple HS,* ULC   10.00
Berkeley, Commercial Bk 10.00
—, —, *brown,* 10.00
—, First Nat Bk, *brown* 10.00
Cedarville, Wells Fargo & Co., T.H. Johnstone, *black, red, (blue)* . .   4.00
Columbia, Wells Fargo & Co., Thomas Conlin, *(green)* 15.00
Farmersville, T.J. Brundage, *black, red,* MLL 10.00
Fresno, Bk of Central California, *(pink)* 8.00
—, Farmer's Nat Bk of Fresno 8.00
—, First Nat Bk, B&R 8.00
—, —, ULC 8.00

Grass Valley, Citizens Bk Agency,
    Pennsylvania Con. Mg. Co., *black, violet HS,* HaL 3.00
Hanford, Farmers & Merchants Bk, ULC 6.00
Hollister, Bk of Hollister 8.00
Jackson, Bk of Amador County, ULC 8.00
Lake Leonard (ms), Wells Fargo & Co., *(blue)* 8.00
Los Angeles, Broadway Bk and Trust Co.,
    Arizona Hay & Grain Co., *black, red,* ULC 15.00
—, Citizens Bk of Los Angeles, R.G. Holabird,
    black, violet HS, (yellow) 10.00
—, Farmers' & Merchants Bk, Western Iron Works, *brown, gray tint*   10.00
—, First Nat Bk, *(blue)* 8.00
—, Los Angeles Nat Bk, ULC 8.00
—, Nat Bk of California,
    Yellow Aster Mining and Milling Co., *black, brown, (blue)* 10.00
Nevada City, Citizens Bk, Mayflower Mining Co., *black, red HS,* IHC   6.00
—, —, *black, red, (pink),* LBC 6.00
—, Agency of Nevada County Bk, *(pink),* Gal 8.00
Oakland, First Nat Bk, *green,* ULC 10.00
Plymouth, Wilmerding-Loewe Co.,
    Rosenward & Kahn, *(blue),* McN 3.00
Redlands, Union Bk of Redlands, HaL 10.00
Sacramento, Nat Bk of D.O. Mills & Co., B&R 6.00
San Bernardino, Farmers Exchange Bk, *brown,* ULC 10.00
—, San Bernardino Nat Bk, *(blue),* ULC 10.00
San Diego, First Nat Bk 10.00
—, Merchants Nat Bk, ULC 8.00
San Francisco, Anglo Californian Bk, *black, gray tint,* Gug 4.00
—, Bk of California, B&R 5.00   5.00
—, —, G.W. McNear, *brown, (blue),* ULC 10.00
—, California Safe Deposit & Trust Co., ULC 4.00
—, Columbian Banking Co., Veterans Home of California, *black, red*   15.00
—, Crocker-Woolworth Nat Bk, *black, gray tint* 3.00
—, —, changed from Tallant Banking Co. (ms) 3.00
—, —, changed from Tallant Banking Co. (paste-over) 3.00
—, —, changed from Tallant Banking Co. (printed over), *black, silver*   3.00
—, First Nat Bk, *(brown)* 7.00
—, Nevada Nat Bk of San Francisco, La Fortuna Mining Co.,
    black, pink tint, B&R 10.00
—, —, Western Sugar Refining Co., *blue, gray tint* 8.00
—, San Francisco Nat Bk, Judson & Shepard, *brown, violet HS* . . .   3.00
—, —, B&R 3.00
—, —, Tallant Banking Co. 3.00
—, Union Trust Co. of San Francisco, *brown, (pink)* 3.00
—, —, *(brown)* 3.00
San Jose, Commercial and Savinga Bk of San Jose, ULC 8.00
Santa Barbara, First Nat Bk 12.00
Taylorsville, J.C. Young, *(brown)* 9.00
Ventura, Bk of Ventura, ULC 10.00
Weaverville, Trinity County Bk changed from C.W. Smith,
    La Grange Hydraulic Gold Mining Co., *black, brown, violet HS*   15.00
Woodland, Farmers & Merchants Bk 10.00
Yreka, Siskiyou County Bk, *(gray),* Cro 10.00

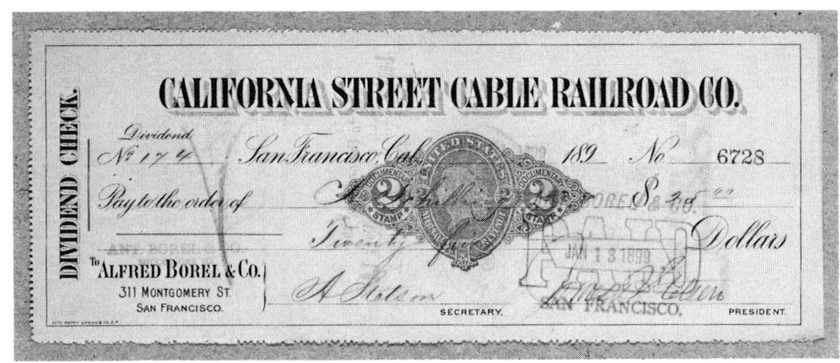

Drafts
Imprint centered

Dixon, Bk of Dixon, *black, tan tint,*		15.00
Fresno, Bk of Central California, ULC............................		12.00
—, —, *black, red, (gray),* ULC.................................		12.00
Hueneme, Bk of Hueneme, *black, red,* ULC......................	15.00	
Long Beach, First Nat Bk of Long Beach, *black, blue,* LAL	18.00	
Los Angeles, Walter Rose, *black, red, (tan)*		15.00
Randsburg, Yellow Aster Mining Co., *black, yellow tint,* ULC.......		10.00
Riverside, First Nat Bk of Riverside, *black, red*		18.00
Sacramento, Nat Bk of D.O. Mills & Co., J.W. Kaseberg, Hal		10.00
San Bernardino, A.M. Ham, *black, brown,* LAL....................		20.00
San Francisco, Anglo Californian Bk, *black, red, brown tint,* ULC...		10.00
—, Bk of California, J. De La Montanya, *black, pink tint,* B&R		7.00
—, California Street Cable Railroad Co., *black, gray tint,* PUC......		20.00
—, California Wine Makers Corporation, *red, blue,*		25.00
San Jose, Whitton & Henderson, *(green)*		10.00

Certificates of Deposit
Imprint centered

Riverside, First Nat Bk, *black, red,* ULC	12.00

Colorado

Type B

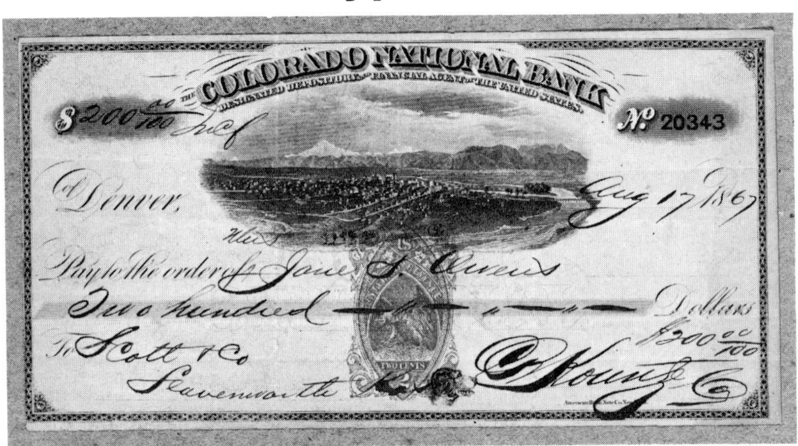

B1 **Orange** [RN-B1]

Drafts
Imprint centered

Central City, Rocky Mountain Nat Bk, WBN	35.00
Denver, Colorado Nat Bk, ABN	85.00

Receipts
Imprint centered

Denver, United States Express Co., *gray*	40.00

Type C

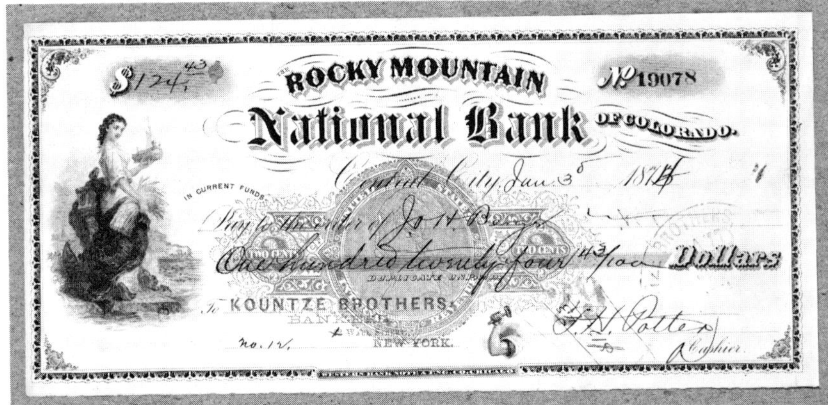

C1 **Orange** [RN-C1]

Drafts
Imprint centered

Central City, Rocky Mountain Nat Bk, *black, blue,* WBN 30.00

Legend below left side of imprint reading:
GOOD ONLY FOR
SIGHT DRAFT.

C11   Brown   **[RN-C11]**

Drafts
Imprint centered

Kit Carson (ms), Otero, Sellar & Co., Tha 65.00

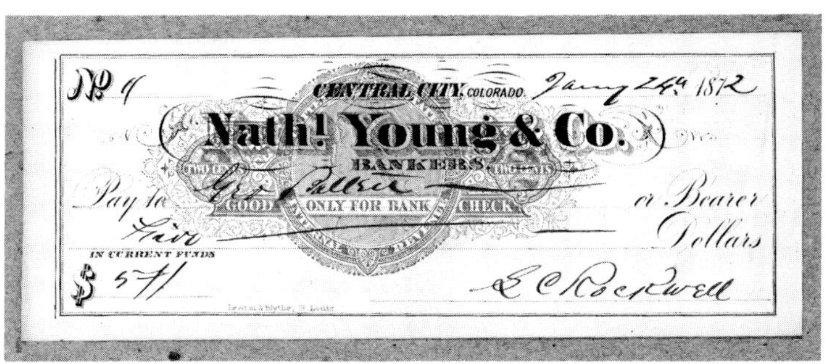

Three part band across lower half of imprint, reading:
GOOD   ONLY FOR BANK   CHECK

C21   Orange   **[RN-C21]**

Checks
Imprint centered

Central City, Nathl. Young & Co., L&B 15.00

Type D

D1   **Orange**   **[RN-D1]**

Checks
Imprint centered

Boulder, Boulder Bk, George C. Corning, CMC	25.00
Denver, First Nat Bk of Denver, WBN	10.00
—, Collins, Snider & Co.,	10.00
Georgetown, First Nat Bk of Georgetown, JWM	20.00

Drafts
Imprint centered

Central City, Rocky Mountain Nat Bk, NBN	35.00
—, —, *black, brown*, NBN	35.00

Type E

E4   **Orange**   **[RN-E4]**

Checks

Imprint centered

Central City, Thatcher, Standley & Co., Bankers, (two settings), CMC   15.00

Type G

G1   **Orange**   **[RN-G1]**

Checks

Imprint centered

Boulder, Nat State Bk of Boulder, CMC	15.00
—, —, *red,* WmM	15.00
—, —, WFM	15.00
Central City, First Nat Bk of Central City, *blue,* WmM	15.00
—, —, *violet,* WmM	15.00
—, Hanington & Mellor, Bankers, *red,* WmM	15.00
Chipeta, Bk of Pitkin County (changed from Miners Exchange Bk, Leadville), *black, blue,* CPH	15.00
Denver, Colorado Nat Bk, WmM	10.00
—, —, *red,* Col	10.00
—, Exchange Bk, CPH	10.00
—, First Nat Bk of Denver,	10.00
Golden, F.E. Everett, Banker, Moore Mining and Smelting Co., Col	15.00
—, L.J. Smith & Co., Bankers, *(blue),* WmM	10.00
Leadville, Bk of Leadville, Col	10.00
—, —, *black, gray tint,* WBN	10.00
—, —, Ward Consolidated Mining Co., WBN	15.00
—, —, J.S.D. Manville, *black, blue,* WBN	10.00
—, First Nat Bk of Leadville, H.H. Tomkins & Co., *black, gray tint,* AGC	15.00
—, Minors' Exchange Bk of Leadville, ✂, WmM	10.00
Trinidad, First Nat Bk, WmM	13.00
—, —, (ms changed from Bk of Southern Colorado), *red,* BBa	15.00

Drafts

Imprint centered

Central City, Rocky Mountain Nat Bk, *black, brown,* NBN	35.00
—, —, *black, gray tint,* CPH	12.00
—, —, *(brown),* Gug	12.00
Colorado Springs, El Paso County Bk, CPH	20.00

As last type, but with imprint printed on the reverse (right side up)

G1a   **Orange**   **[RN-G1a]**

Drafts
Imprint centered

Leadville, Manville & McCarthy, ...   30.00

Type H

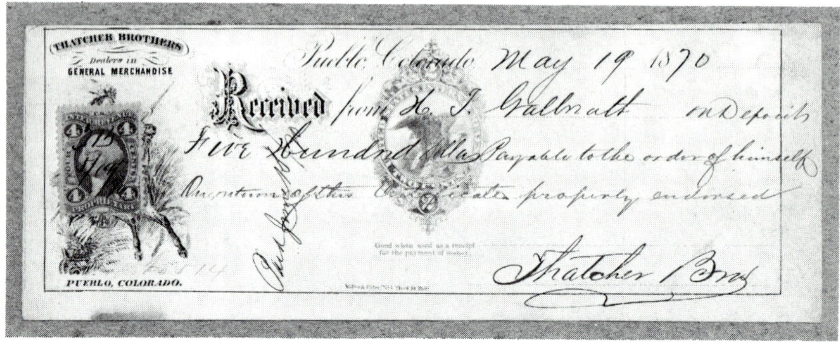

Typeset legend centered below imprint, reading:
Good when used as a receipt
for the payment of money.
Legend printed separately from imprint

H7   **Orange, with yellow legend**   **[RN-H3c var]**

Certificate of Deposit *(changed from a receipt)*
Imprint centered

Pueblo, Thatcher Brothers,
(an additional 1st Issue revenue added) MEI   1000-

Type K

K4   **Gray**   **[RN-K4]**

Checks
Imprint centered

Cañon City, Fremont County Bk, WFM 75.00

Type M

M2 **Orange** [RN-M2]

Checks
Imprint centered

Denver, Collins, Snider & Co., CSS 60.00

Type P

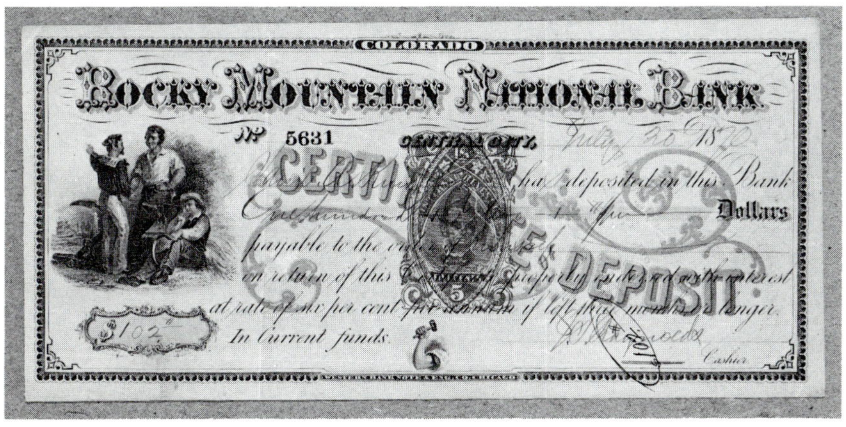

P5 **Orange** [RN-P5]

Certificates of Deposit
Imprint left

Denver, Colorado Nat Bk, ABN 100.00

Imprint centered

Central City, Rocky Mountain Nat Bk, *black, green,* WBN 35.00

Type Q

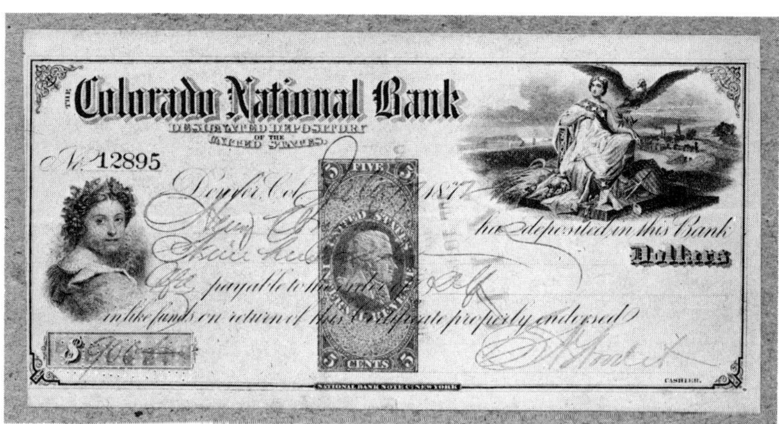

Q1   Orange   **[RN-Q1]**

Certificates of Deposit
Imprint centered

Central City, Rocky Mountain Nat Bk, *black, green,* WBN . . . . ▸   125.00
Denver, Colorado Nat Bk, NBN 100.00

Type X

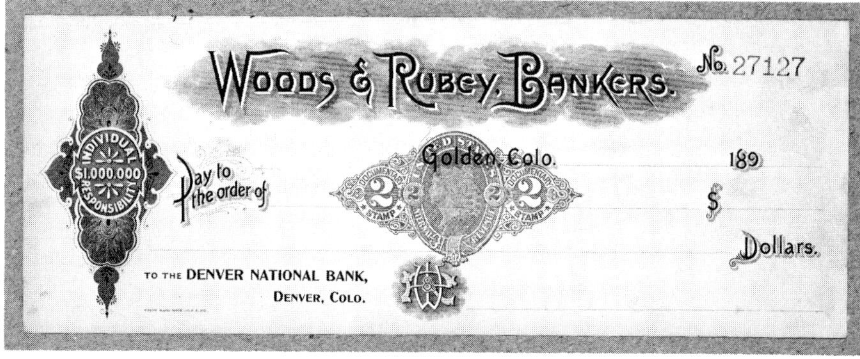

X7   Orange   **[RN-X7]**

Checks
Imprint centered

Boulder, Nat State Bk, bk name in script, PSC. 8.00
—, —, bk name in roman type, PSC 8.00
Cañon City, Fremont County Bk, *green,* Pue 12.00
Central City, Rocky Mountain Nat Bk,
    Kansas-Burroughs Consolidated Mining Co., *black, black tint,* DLC   10.00

Colorado Springs, Exchange Nat Bk, Hal 8.00
—, First Nat Bk, Out 10.00
Cripple Creek, First Nat Bk, Pue 10.00
—, —, *(green)*, Hal 10.00
—, —, Centennial Gold Extraction Co., Pue 15.00
—, —, Sternberger-Siegel Brokerage Co., *(green)*, Pue 10.00
Denver, Central Savings Bk,
    Equitable Coal Mining & Mercantile Co., *(green)*, MCJ 10.00
—, Denver Nat Bk, ... 10.00
—, —, *(yellow)*, MCJ 7.00
—, —, *(pink)*, MCJ 7.00
—, Denver Savings Bk, MCJ 8.00
Georgetown, Bk of Georgetown, PSC 10.00
Gunnison, First Nat Bk of Gunnison, Murray Bros.,
    black, red, (blue), Pue 18.00

Drafts
Imprint centered

Aspen, Harry G. Koch, *brown,* Pue 18.00
Colorado Springs, DeBerry & Powell, *(green),* 10.00
Denver, Vindicator Consolidated Gold Mining Co., *black, red,* Pue . . 15.00
Golden, Woods & Rubey, *black, red,* UBN 15.00

Certificates of Deposit
Imprint centered

Cripple Creek, First Nat Bk, WFR 20.00

Type X

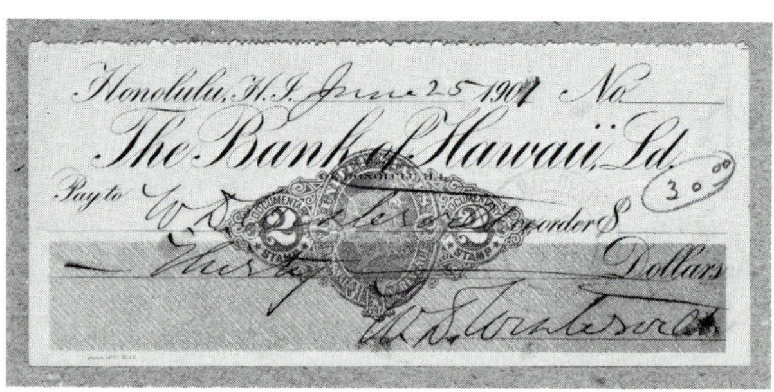

X7   **Orange**   **[RN-X7]**

Checks
Imprint centered

Honolulu, Bk of Hawaii, Ltd, *(pale green)*, ULC 110.00

Idaho

Type C

Three part band across lower half of imprint, reading:

GOOD   **ONLY FOR BANK**   **CHECK**

C21   **Orange**   **[RN-C21]**

Checks
Imprint centered

Silver City, Wells, Fargo & Co., Owyhee Mining Co., ...   80.00

Type G

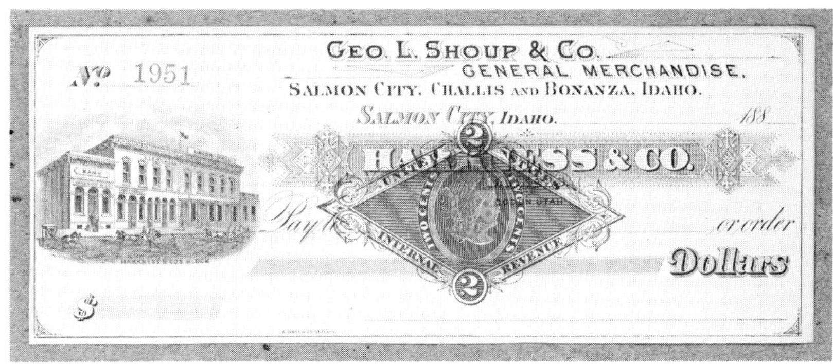

G1   **Orange**   **[RN-G1]**

Checks
Imprint centered

Salmon City, Harkness & Co., Bankers,
    Geo. L. Shoup & Co., *black, gray tint,* AGC 25.00
—, —, *blue-black, pink tint,* AGC 30.00   25.00

Terminus of the Northⁿ. R.R.,
   Banking House of Fred. J. Kiesel & Co., JHa 40.00

Type X

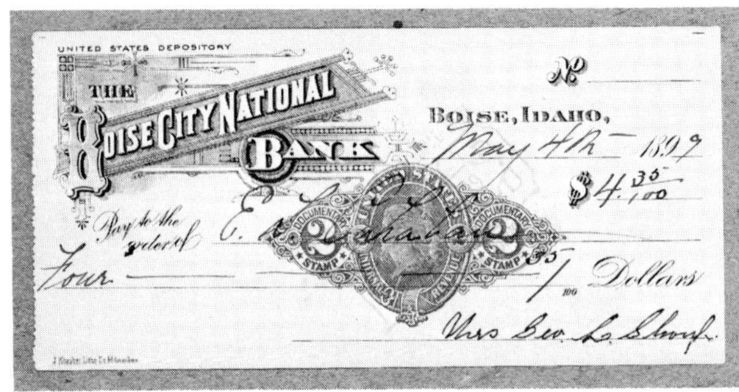

X7   **Orange**   **[RN-X7]**

Checks
Imprint centered

Boise, Bk of Commerce, GDB 10.00
—, Boise City Nat Bk, K&C 10.00
—, Capital State Bk, *(blue)*, Hal 8.00
—, —, Loree & Frantz Hardware Co., (Co. name at left), *(pink)*, AGC   8.00
—, —, (Co. name at signature line), *(pink)*, AGC 8.00
—, First Nat Bk of Idaho, *red*, Hal 8.00
Salmon City, McCornick & Co., Bankers, Geo. L. Shoup & Co., SLL   15.00

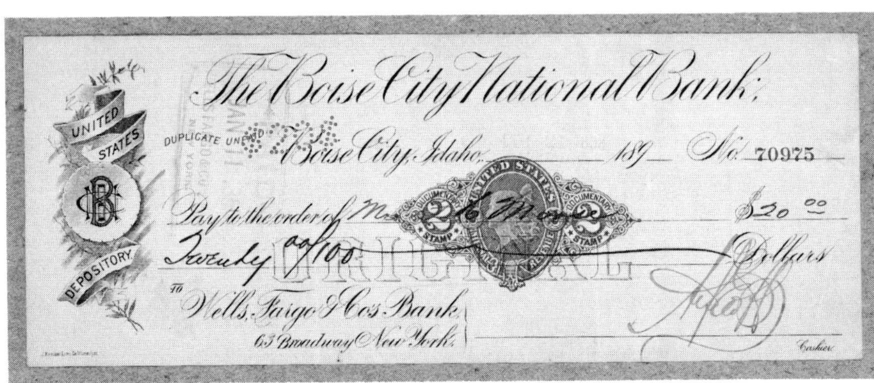

Drafts
Imprint centered

Boise City, Boise City Nat Bk, *black, pink tint*, K&C 12.00

H.J.W. Daugherty

PHILATELIC AUCTIONS
P.O. Box 1146
Eastham, Mass. 02642
(508) 255-7488

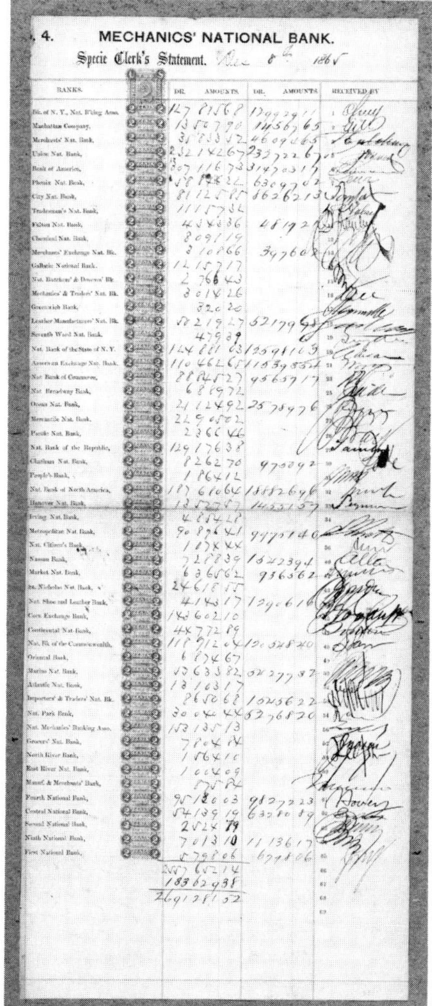

Write For Our Latest Catalogue
Revenues Are Always Included

Montana

Type B

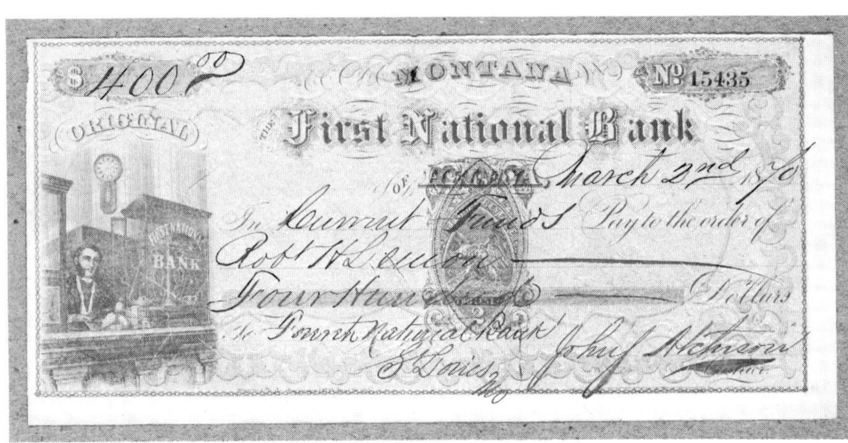

B1   Orange   **[RN-B1]**

Drafts

Imprint centered

Helena, First Nat Bk, *green, yellow-green tint,* S&B 100.00
—, L.H. Hershfield & Bro., RFM. 25.00
Virginia City, L.H. Hershfield & Co., M&H. 25.00

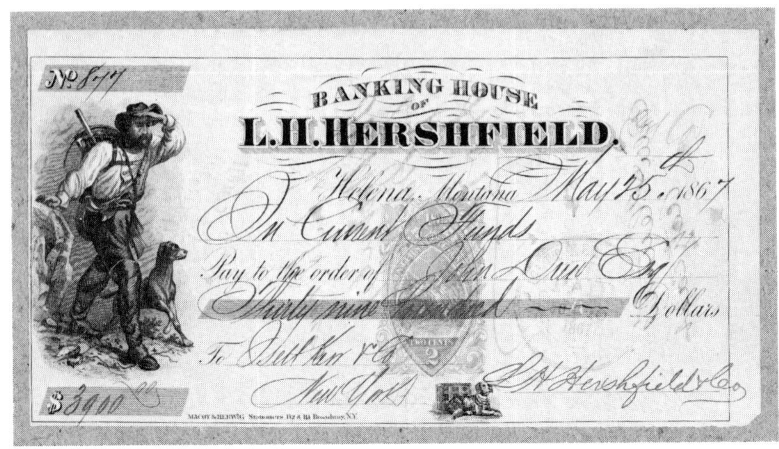

B6   Green   **[RN-B6]**

Drafts

Imprint centered

Helena, L.H. Hershfield, M&H. 60.00

Type C

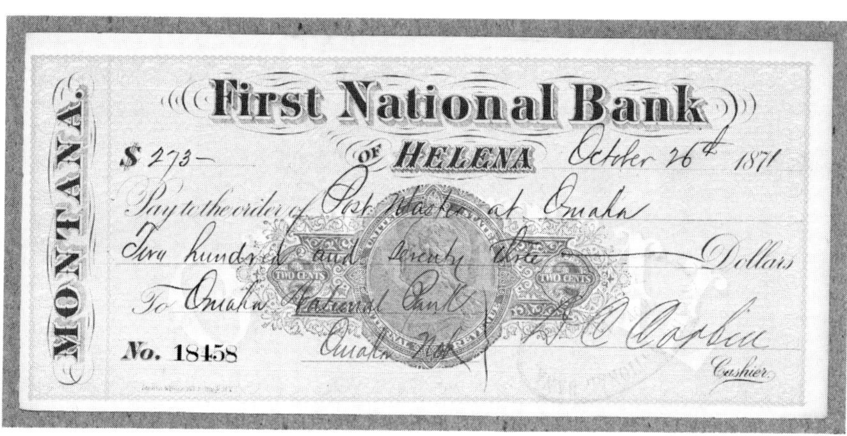

C1   Orange   **[RN-C1]**

Drafts
Imprint centered

Helena, First Nat Bk, *brown, purple tint,* S&B 25.00
—, —, *brown, olive tint,* S&B 25.00

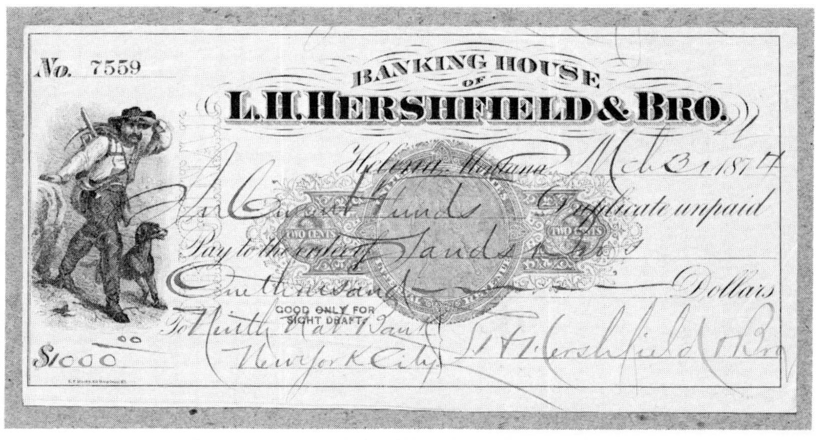

Legend below left side of imprint reading:
GOOD ONLY FOR
SIGHT DRAFT

C13   Orange   **[RN-C13]**

Drafts
Imprint centered

Helena, L.H. Hershfield & Bro., *black, red,* RFM 35.00

Type D

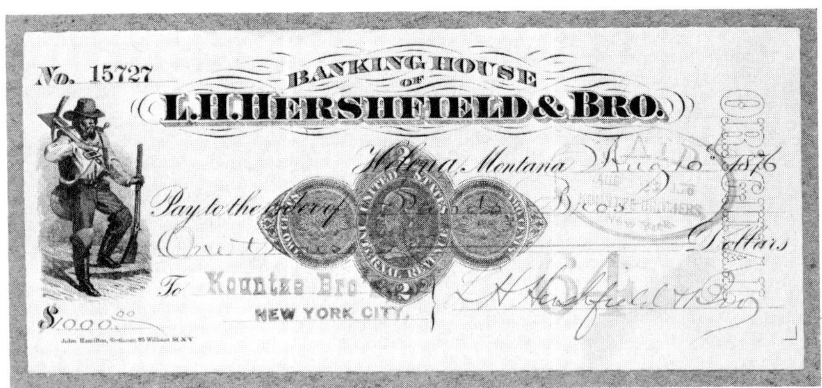

D1   **Orange**   **[RN-D1]**

Checks
Imprint centered

Helena, L.H. Hershfield & Bro., *red*, CMC 10.00

Drafts
Imprint centered

Helena, L.H. Hershfield & Bro., (no vign.), *black, blue*, JHa 12.00
—, —, vign. of miner, *black, red, violet HS*, JHa 15.00
—, First Nat Bk, *brown, violet tint*, W&B 25.00

Legend below left side of imprint reading:
GOOD ONLY FOR
SIGHT DRAFT

D9   **Orange**   **[RN-D9]**

Drafts
Imprint centered

Helena, L.H. Hershfield & Bro., *black, red, gold,* RFM 50.00

Type E

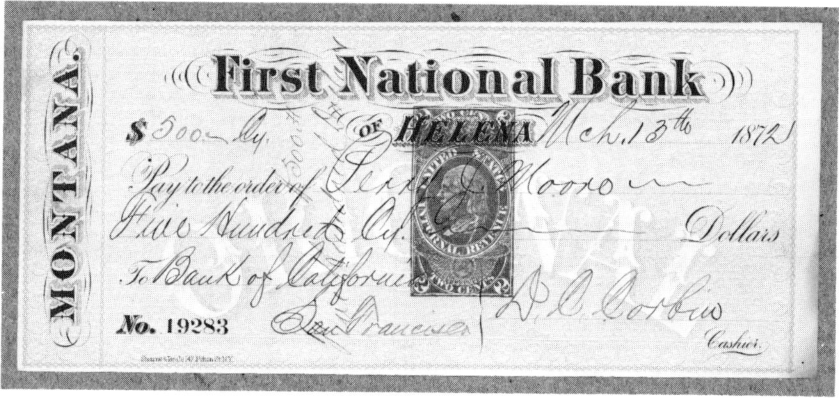

E4   **Orange**   **[RN-E4]**

Drafts
Imprint centered

Helena, First Nat Bk of Helena, *brown, gray tint,* S&B 30.00

Type F

F1   **Orange**   **[RN-F1]**

Checks
Imprint centered

Helena, P. Hayden & Co. (ms changed from
Peoples Nat Bk of Helena), CMC. 10.00

Type G

G1   **Orange**   **[RN-G1]**

Checks
Imprint centered

Butte, Donnell, Clark & Larabie,	
Colorado and Montana Smelting Co., *red,* WmM	10.00
—, First Nat Bk of Butte, Butte Hardware Co., *green, violet HS,* B&K	20.00
—, S.T. Hauser & Co., vign. of miner, Cly	8.00
—, —, no vign., Cly	8.00
—, —, HCK	8.00
—, —, ornate floral block at left, HCK	8.00
Glendale, N. Armstrong & Co., BBa	25.00
—, —, Hecla Consolidated Mining Co.,	25.00
Helena, First Nat Bk of Helena, vign. of miner, Cly	12.00
—, —, PLC	12.00
—, —, *blue,* Cly	12.00
—, —, 'MONTANA' at left, reading up, B&K	10.00
—, —, *(brown),* C&R	10.00
—, —, *black, violet tint,* WmM	12.00
—, —, A.M. Holter & Bro., C&R	12.00
—, L.H. Hershfield & Bro., *violet,* CMC	10.00
—, —, 'Montana' at left, reading up, *violet,* CMC	10.00
—, —, *red,* CMC	10.00
—, Second Nat Bk, *black, gray tint,* K&C ➤	8.00

Drafts
Imprint centered

Butte, Butte City Bk, S.T. Hauser & Co., *brown, violet tint,* PLC	25.00
—, First Nat Bk, *black, deep blue, violet HS,* StL	20.00
—, S.T. Hauser & Co., *brown, violet tint,* HCK	25.00
—, —, *brown, purple HS, gray tint,* HCK	25.00
—, —, C&R	25.00
—, —, PLC	25.00
Deer Lodge, Donnell, Clark & Larabie, WBN.	45.00
—, —, NNW	23.00

—, First Nat Bk, WBN 35.00
Helena, First Nat Bk of Helena, *brown, violet*, PLC............... 25.00
—, —, *black, brown tint*, CMC.................................. 25.00
—, —, *blue, red, olive tint*, C&R 30.00
—, L.H. Hershfield & Bro., *black, red, violet HS*, JHa 15.00
—, —, *black, red*, CMC... 15.00
Merchants Nat Bk, *black, red, (light brown)*, CMC................ 14.00

Bills of Exchange
Imprint centered

Helena, L.H. Hershfield & Brother, *black, red*, ABN 35.00

Type K

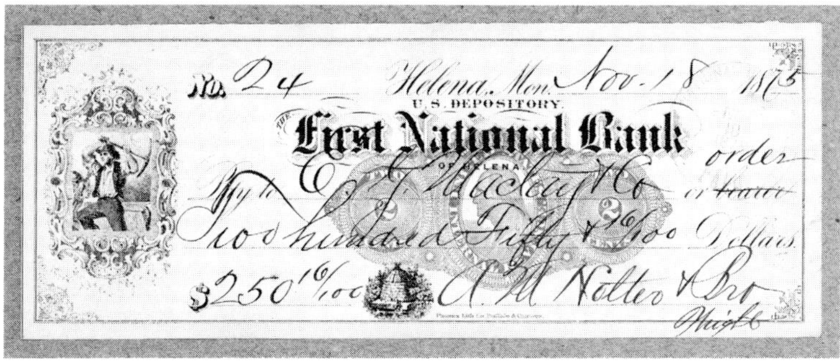

K5   **Orange**   **[RN-K5]**

Checks
Imprint centered

Helena, First Nat Bk, PLC..................................... 50.00

Type X

X7   **Orange**   **[RN-X7]**

Checks
Imprint centered

Dillon, First Nat Bk, S.S. Patterson, *brown, red, (yellow),* Hal. 12.00
Helena, American Nat Bk, A.M. Holter Hardware Co.,
    (pale yellow), WBN 13.00
Marysville, Montana Nat Bk, Montana Mining Co., WBN 14.00
Virginia City, Hall & Bennett, T&J 12.00
White Sulphur Springs, First Nat Bk, J.T. Elston, *black, gray tint,* GDB   14.00

Drafts
Imprint centered

Browning, J.H. Sherburne, UBN. 20.00
Helena, A.M. Holter Hardware Co., *black, red-brown,* Bla 12.00
Pony, Isdell Mercantile Co., *black, red, gray tint,* CPC 15.00
Walkerville, Alice Gold & Silver Mining Co., *black, red,* UtL 20.00

Nevada

Type B

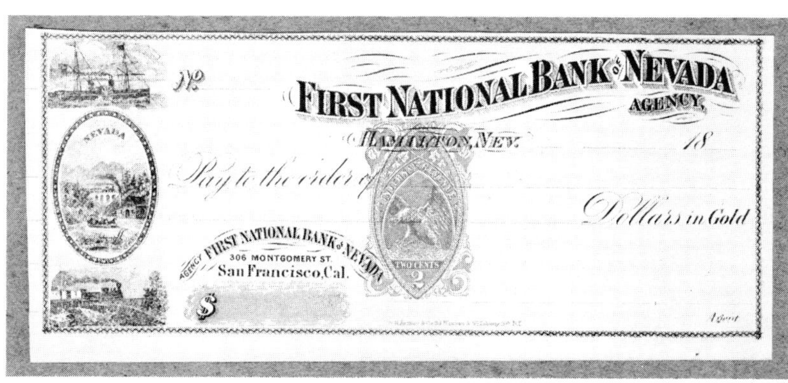

B1   Orange   **[RN-B1]**

Checks
Imprint centered

Hamilton, First Nat Bk of Nevada Agency, *red,* WHA 30.00

Drafts
Imprint centered

Hamilton, First Nat Bk of Nevada Agency, *red,* WHA 30.00

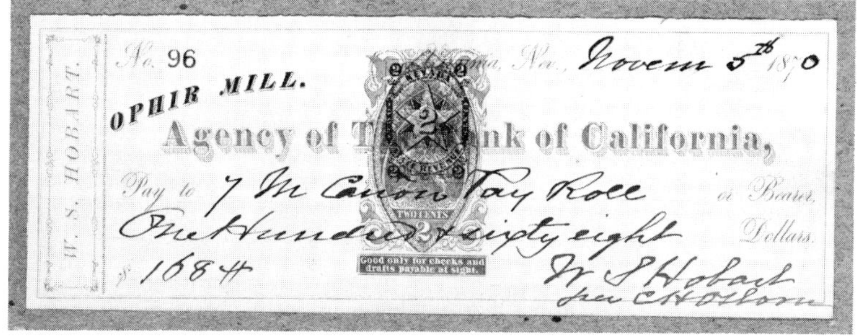

Rectangular tablet below imprint, reading:

**Good only for checks and
drafts payable at sight.**

With additional 2 Cent Nevada revenue imprint

B16A   Orange, with Red-Orange Nevada imprint   **[RN-B16a]**

Checks

Both imprints centered,
Nevada superimposed on Federal

Virginia, Agency of the Bk of California, (no user)................375.00
—, —, Ophir Mill, W.S. Hobart, *red, blue*........................   325.00
—, —, Mariposa Mill Co., *brown, blue* 325.00

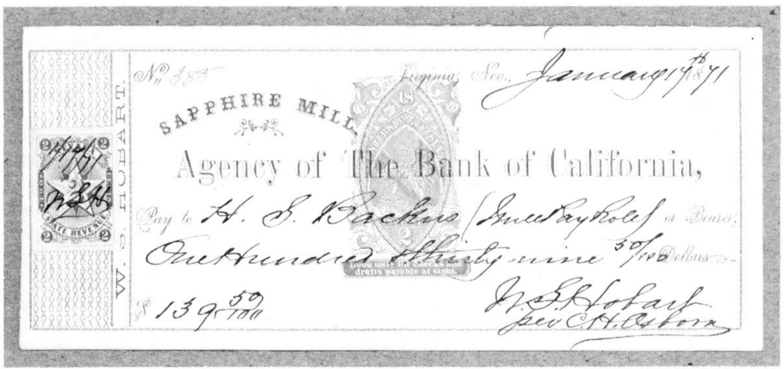

Octagonal tablet below imprint, reading:

**Good only for checks and
drafts payable at sight.**

B17   Orange   **[RN-B17]**

Checks

Imprint centered

Virginia, Agency of the Bk of California, (No user)................   20.00
—, —, Sapphire Mill, W.S. Hobart, *blue*........................   22.50

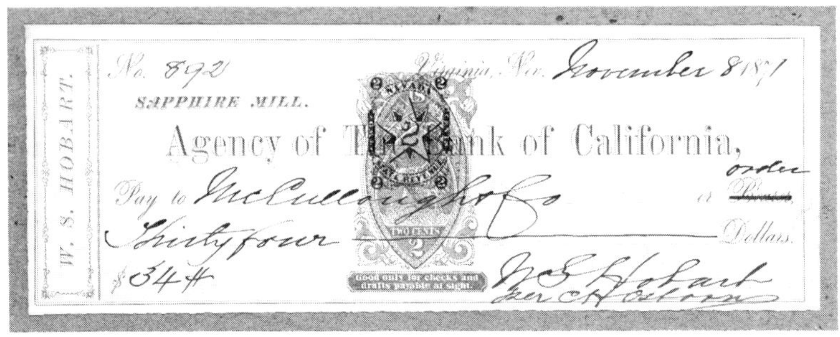

As last type, with additional 2 Cent Nevada revenue imprint

B18   Orange, with Red-Orange Nevada imprint   **[RN-B17b]**

Checks
Both imprints centered,
Nevada superimposed on Federal

Virginia, Agency of the Bk of California,
  Gould and Curry Silver Mining Co., *green* 35.00
 —, —, Hale & Norcross Silver Mining Co., *red* 200.00
 —, —, Sapphire Mill, W.S. Hobart, *blue* 150.00

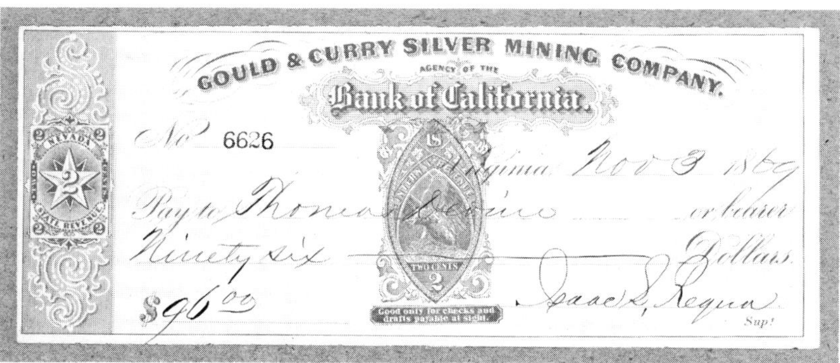

B19   **Orange, with Green Nevada imprint**   **[RN-B17c]**

Checks
Federal imprint centered, Nevada imprint to left

Virginia, Agency of the Bk of California,
  Gould and Curry Silver Mining Co., *green* 40.00

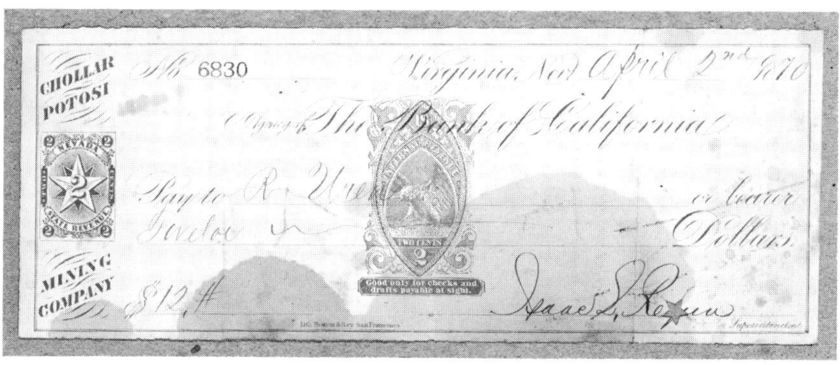

B19A   **Orange, with Violet Nevada imprint**   **[RN-B17d]**

Checks
Federal imprint centered, Nevada imprint to left

Virginia, Agency of the Bk of California,
  Chollar Potosi Mining Co., *violet,* B&R   1500-

Type C

C1   Orange   **[RN-C1]**

Bills of Exchange
Imprint centered

Austin, Agency of the Manhattan Silver Mining Co. of Nevada, H&C   50.00

Three part band across lower half of imprint, reading:

GOOD   ONLY FOR BANK   CHECK

C21   Orange   **[RN-C21]**

Checks
Imprint centered

Virginia, Agency of the Bk of California, Bacon Mill, *black, violet*. . .   25.00
—, —, Gould & Curry Silver Mining Co., *green* 10.00
—, —, additional NV adhesive added. 15.00
—, —, Hale and Norcross, ✂, *red* 25.00
—, —, Mariposa Mill Co., *brown, violet* 25.00
—, —, Trench Mill, *black, violet* 25.00

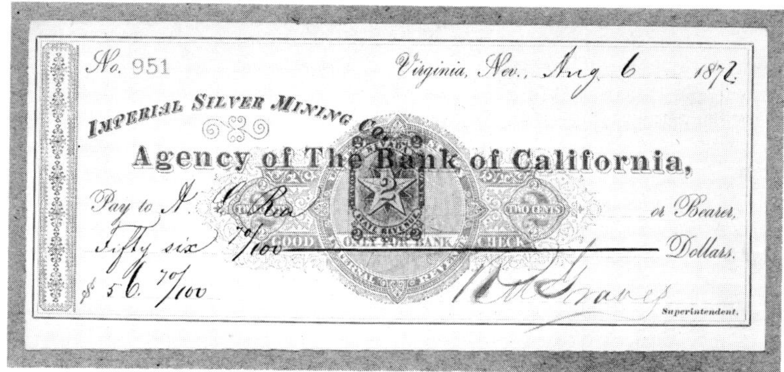

As last type, with additional 2 Cent Nevada revenue imprint

C24   Orange, with Red-Orange Nevada imprint   [RN-C21b]
Checks
**Both imprints centered,
Nevada superimposed on Federal**

Virginia, Agency of the Bk of California,
   Gould & Curry Silver Mining Co., *green* 30.00
—, Imperial Silver Mining Co., *green* 75.00
—, Occidental Mill, *blue*.. 75.00
—, Pac. Mill & Mng Co.
   (ms changed from Occidental Mill), *blue, red ms* 75.00 75.00

Type D

D1   Orange   [RN-D1]
Checks
Imprint centered

Austin, Paxton & Curtis, EDC.................................... 10.00
Carson, Carson City Savings Bk, *black, violet HS*................ 12.50
—, —, Wells, Fargo & Co., (no user), *blue*...................... 15.00
—, —, Bac 15.00

—, —, J.W. Haynie & Co., *blue*, Bac. 15.00
—, —, El Dorado Wood & Flume Co. 15.00
Eureka, D.B. Immel & Co., HaP 15.00
—, Paxton & Co., ALB 15.00
—, —, Ban 12.00
Virginia, Agency of the Bk of California, (no user), ... 15.00
—, —, CMC 15.00
—, —, Bacon Mill, *black, violet* 20.00
—, —, Best & Belcher Mng. Co.
    (ms changed from Trench Mill), *black, purple, red ms* 15.00
—, —, Carson and Tahoe Lumber and Fluming Co., *red* 15.00
—, —, Chollar Potosi Mining Co., *violet*, B&R. 30.00
—, —, Consolidated Mill, *blue* 20.00 15.00
—, —, Gould & Curry Silver Mining Co., *green* 10.00
—, —, Imperial Silver Mining Co., *green* 15.00
—, —, Pacific Mill & Mining Co., *green*. 15.00
—, —, Sacramento Mill, *blue* 20.00
—, —, Sapphire Mill, W.S. Hobart, *blue*. 15.00
—, —, Trench Mill, *black, purple* 20.00
—, —, Virginia & Truckee Railroad Co., *blue* 15.00
—, —, Woodworth Mill, *blue, red*. 15.00
—, Bullion & Ex. Bk, (HS changed from Agency of the
    Bk of California), Ludwig Copper M. Co. (ms changed from
    Devil's Gate Mill), *black, red ms, blue HS, pink tint*, AJL 30.00

Drafts
Imprint centered

Austin, Manhattan Silver Mining Co. of Nevada,
    violet, EDC (2 settings) 3.00
Gold Hill, Agency of the Bk of California, *blue*, B&R. 14.00

Scrip taxed as Drafts
Imprint centered

Austin, Manhattan Silver Mining Co., 1 Dollar, *black*, M&K 35.00
—, —, 3 Dollars, *brown*, M&K 100.00
—, —, 5 Dollars, *green*, M&K. 35.00
—, —, 10 Dollars, *blue*, M&K 35.00

—, —, 20 Dollars, *brown,* M&K 35.00
—, —, 50 Dollars, *red,* M&K.................................... 100.00
—, —, 100 Dollars, *orange,* M&K 100.00

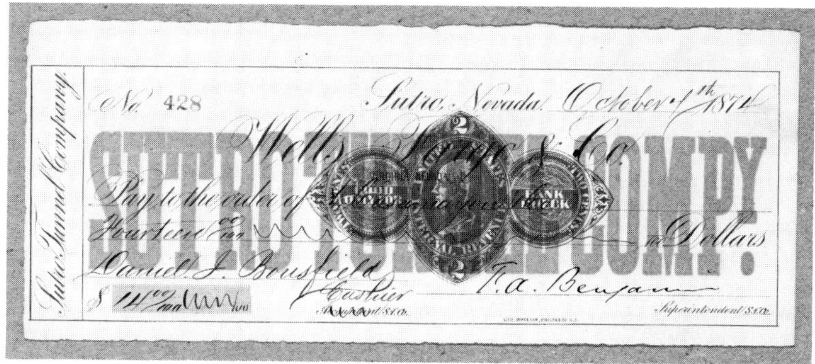

Legend to left and right, within circles of imprint, reading:

GOOD	**BANK**
ONLY FOR	**CHECK**

D7 Orange   [RN-D7]

Checks
Imprint centered

Austin (ms), Bk of California, *green, yellow tint* 18.00
Sutro, Wells, Fargo & Co., Sutro Tunnel Co., *black, tan,* WhP....... 50.00
Virginia, Agency of the Bk of California,
    Hale and Norcross Silver Mining Co., *red* 20.00
—, —, Haynie & Co., *black, red* 18.00
—, —, Imperial Silver Mining Co., *green* 20.00

Drafts (improper use)
Imprint centered

Austin, Manhattan Silver Mining Co. of Nevada, *violet,* EDC........   7.50

Type E

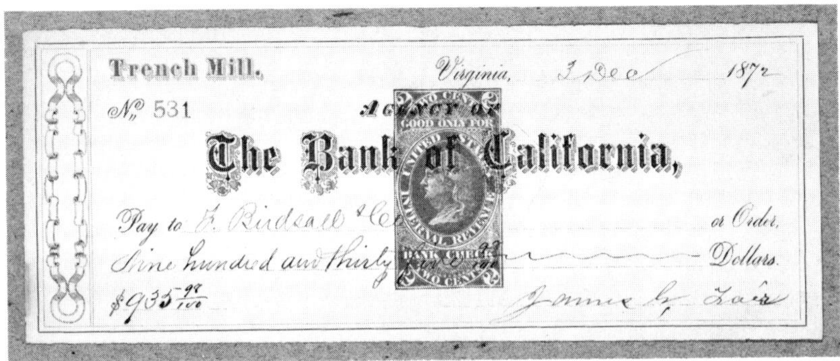

Legend within imprint, above and below portrait, reading:

**GOOD ONLY FOR
BANK CHECK**

E7   **Orange**   **[RN-E7]**

Checks
Imprint centered

Carson, Wells, Fargo & Co., J.W. Haynie & Co., *blue,* Bac 25.00
Virginia, Agency of the Bk of California, Bacon Mill, *black, violet*. . .   20.00
—, —, Gould & Curry Silver Mining Co., *green* 20.00
—, —, Mariposa Mill Co., *brown, red* 25.00
—, —, Trench Mill, *black, violet* 25.00
—, —, Woodworth Mill, *red, blue*. 20.00

Drafts (improper use)
Imprint centered

Austin (ms), Manhattan Silver Mining Co., *violet,* EDC 20.00

Type F

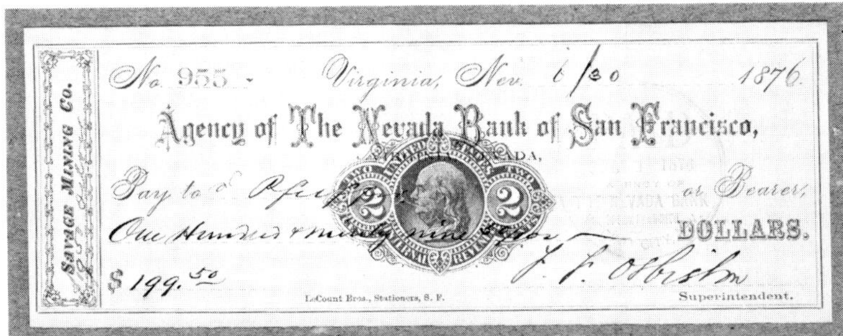

F1   **Orange**   **[RN-F1]**

Checks
Imprint centered

Carson, Carson City Savings Bk, *black, black tint,* E&K 10.00
—, —, Merchants' Exchange Bk, *black, purple HS,* Kre 15.00
Eureka, D.B. Immel & Co., HaP 15.00
Virginia, Agency of the Bk of California, Vivian Mining Co., *red* 20.00
—, Agency of the Nevada Bk of San Francisco, (no user), B&R 15.00
—, —, *brown,* B&R 15.00
—, —, Eagle Salt Works, *black, violet HS,* B&R 15.00
—, —, Savage Mining Co., *red,* LBr 15.00

Drafts
Imprint centered

Austin, Manhattan Silver Mining Co., *violet,* EDC 5.00

Type G

G1   **Orange**   **[RN-G1]**

Checks
Imprint centered

Austin, Paxton & Curtis, WmM 5.00
—, —, Manhattan S.M. Co., *black, violet HS,* WmM 5.00
Carson, Carson City Savings Bk, *black, black tint,* Kre 12.00
—, —, *(brown),* Kre 20.00
, First Nat Bk of Reno, Chilled Car Wheel Gringing Co., *(brown)*   25.00
—, Wells Fargo & Co., CMC 10.00
—, —, Parker & Tobey, *purple,* Ban 20.00
—, —, H.M. Yerington, *blue,* Bac 25.00
—, Wells Fargo & Co's Bk, Cro 12.50
—, —, Mutual Benefit Association of the V. & T. R. R., *red,* Bac 20.00
—, —, H.M. Yerington, *blue,* Bac 15.00
Eureka, Paxton & Co. (2 settings) 8.00
—, —, changed from D.B. Immel & Co., *black, red,* HaP 12.00
—, —, Hiram Johnson 10.00

Gold Hill, Agency of the Bk of California,
    Belcher Silver Mining Co., *(brown),* AJL. 25.00
—, Agency of the Nevada Bk of S.F.,
    Yellow Jacket Silver Mining Co., *red, blue* 25.00
Hamilton, White Pine County Bk,
    Eberhardt & Aurora Mining Co., *green,* ALB. 35.00
Ophir, First Nat Bk, Washoe-Ophir Tailings Co., *(light brown)* 20.00
—, —, PUC 20.00
Reno, D.A.Bender & Co., *red* 18.00
—, —, First Nat Bk, *(brown)*. 18.00
—, Paxton, Curtis & Co., ALB 25.00
Tybo, Daniel Meyer, Tybo Cons. Mining Co.. . . . . 35.00
Virginia, Agency of the Bk of California, *(blue),* CMC 6.00
—, —, Belcher Silver Mining Co., *blue* 20.00
—, —, Carson and Tahoe Lumber and Fluming Co., *red* 15.00
—, —, Chollar-Norcross-Savage-Shaft-Co., *blue, (pink),* AJL 20.00
—, —, Consolidated Imperial Mining Co., AJL 20.00
—, —, Virginia & Truckee Railroad Co., B&R 20.00
—, —, changed from the Nevada Bk of San Francisco,
    Savage Mining Co., *red,* LBr 14.00
—, —, H.M. Yerington, *blue,* B&R 20.00
—, Agency of the Nevada Bk of San Francisco, *brown,* B&R 15.00
—, —, Bacon Mill, *blue,* B&R 35.00
—, —, Best & Belcher Mining Co., *blue,* B&R. 20.00
—, —, Gould & Curry Silver Mining Co., *blue,* B&R 15.00
—, —, Gould & Curry & Best & Belcher Joint Shaft, *brown,* GTB . . . 22.00
—, —, Hale & Norcross Silver Mining Co., *blue,* B&R. 20.00
—, —, North Con. Virginia Mining Co. 20.00
—, —, Pacific Mill & Mining Co., *blue,* B&R. 20.00
—, —, (HS changed from Bacon Mill, *blue, violet HS,* B&R. 20.00
—, —, (HS changed from Morgan Mill, *blue, violet HS,* B&R 25.00
—, —, (HS changed from Trench Mill, *blue, violet HS,* B&R 15.00
—, —, Pacific Wood, Lumber & Flume Co., *blue,* B&R. 25.00
—, —, Sacramento Mill, *blue,* B&R. 25.00
—, —, Savage Mining Co., *red,* LBr 15.00
—, —, Sierra Nevada Mexican and Union Shaft Co., *green,* ALB . . . 25.00
—, —, S.N.M.U. Shaft Co., (HS changed from
    North Con. Virginia Mining Co.), *black, violet HS*. 20.00
—, —, Sierra Nevada Wood & Lumber Co., *pale violet,* ECP 15.00
—, —, *violet,* B&R. 17.50
—, Bk of California (ms changed from Wells Fargo & Co's Bk), Bac 15.00
—, Wells, Fargo & Co's Bk, Savage Mining Co., *violet,* Bac. 15.00
—, —, *purple,* FBo. 15.00
Washoe City (ms changed from Sacramento),
    Nat Gold Bk of D.O. Mills, *(brown)* 35.00

Drafts

Imprint centered

Austin, Gage, Curtis & Co., Manhattan Silver Mining Co., *violet* 3.00
—, —, *purple* (2 settings) 3.00
—, —, *violet,* EDC. 3.00
—, Manhattan Silver Mining Co., *violet,* EDC (2 settings) 3.00
—, —, *purple,* EDC 3.00

—, —, *violet,* WmM... 3.00
—, —, *violet,* M&K 3.00
—, —, *purple,* M&K 3.00
Carson, Carson City Savings Bk, *black, violet HS, (brown),* Kre 10.00
—, —, *black, (lilac),* Kre 10.00
—, —, same but 'SILVER,' *black, violet HS, (lilac),* Kre 10.00

Type X

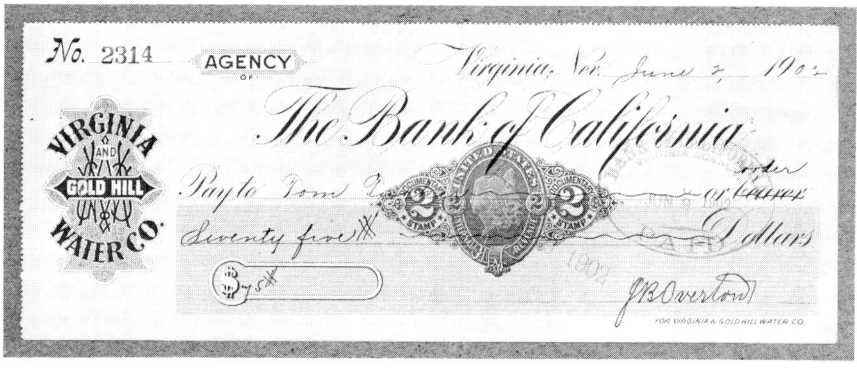

X7   Orange   [RN-X7]

Checks
Imprint centered

Carson, Bullion and Exchange Bk, *(pale pink),* IHC 12.00
—, —, *brown,* H&O 12.00
Virginia, Agency of the Bk of California,
    Carson and Tahoe Lumber and Fluming Co., *black, pink tint,* B&R   6.00
—, —, Comstock Pumping Association, *(gray)*.................. 12.00
—, —, Consolidated California and Virginia Mining Co.,
    blue, pink tint... 6.00
—, —, Ophir Silver Mining Co., *blue, (tan),* B&P 7.50
—, —, Virginia and Gold Hill Water Co., *blue* 20.00

Drafts
Imprint centered

Carson, Bullion and Exchange Bk, *black, violet HS,* LBr 10.00
—, —, *black, yellow tint,* IHC.................................. 10.00
—, —, *black, pale yellow tint,* ULC............................. 10.00
—, —, *black, gold, pale gray tint,* IHC.......................... 10.00

Certificates of Deposit
Imprint centered

Carson, Bullion and Exchange Bk, *black, pink tint,* IHC............ 10.00

New Mexico

Type G

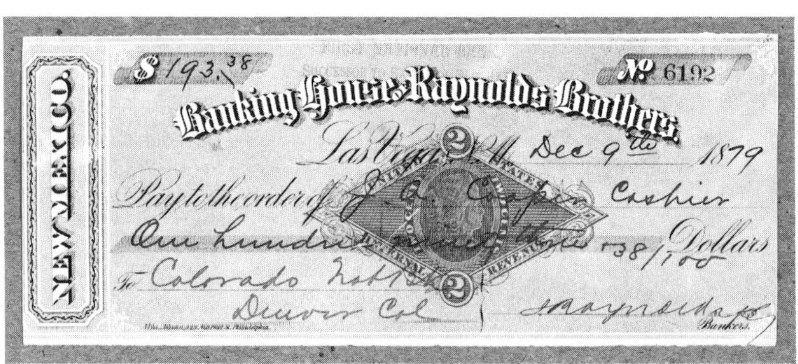

G1   **Orange**   [RN-G1]

Checks
Imprint centered

Carlisle Mines, Bk of C.P. Crawford, Carlisle Mining Co., H&S	35.00
Silver City, C.P. Crawford,	
(ms changed from H.M. Porter), *red,* HRH	20.00
—, Meredith & Ailman,	35.00
—, Porter and Crawford, *red,* CMC	20.00

Drafts
Imprint centered

Las Vegas, First Nat Bk, changed from	
Raynolds Brothers (handstamped), *black, black tint,* WmM	30.00

Type X

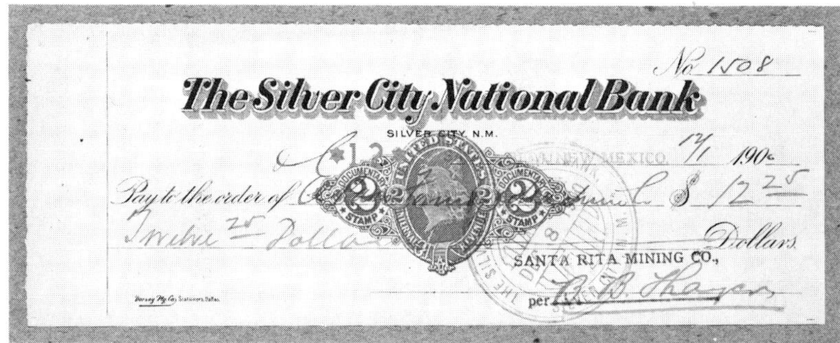

X7   **Orange**   [RN-X7]

Checks
Imprint centered

Santa Rita, Silver City Nat Bk, Santa Rita Mining Co., *black, violet,* DPC   10.00
Silver City, Silver City Nat Bk, Clk 10.00

Certificates

Bonds

Maxwell Land Grant and Railway Co., £100 or 1200 guilders 7% first mortgage bond. This bond does not pay in the U.S.A.! Issue of 7,000, dated 13 June, 1870. 50 coupons attached. Imprints: V4, P5 centered on face; P5 on reverse; Dutch 75 centimes handstamp on face, to right; English 2 shillings 6 pence embossed revenue on face, to the left of UNITED in the title of the bond. *black, brown,* NBN   1000-

Oregon

Type B

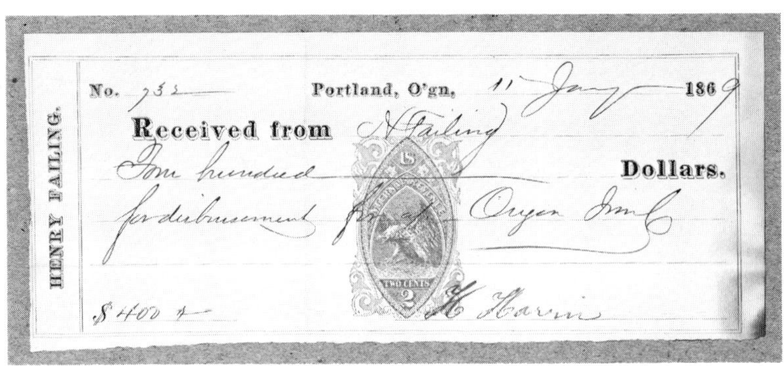

B1   Orange   [RN-B1]

Receipts
Imprint centered

Portland, Henry Failing, ... 15.00

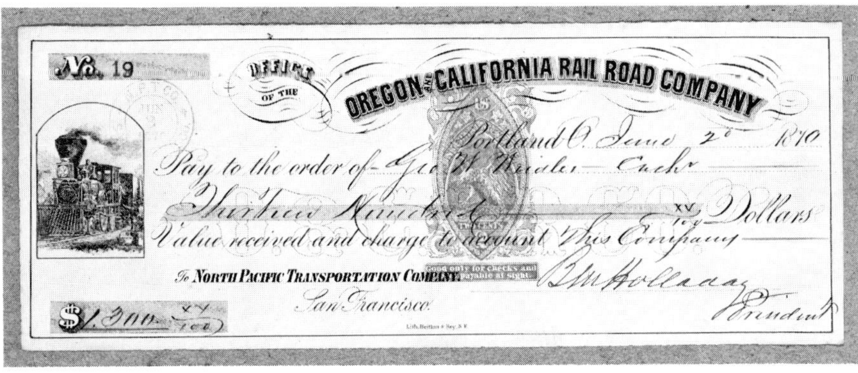

Rectangular tablet below imprint, reading:
**Good only for checks and
drafts payable at sight.**

B16   Orange   [RN-B16]

Drafts
Imprint centered

Portland, Oregon and California Rail Road Co., B&R 40.00
—, —, same, signature of Ben Holladay 75.00

Octagonal tablet below imprint, reading:
**Good when issued for the
payment of money.**

B20   Orange   **[RN-B20]**

Checks *(improper use)*
Imprint centered

First Nat Bk of Portland (ms), H.W. Corbett & Co., *violet,* CMC 10.00
—, —, Henry Failing, EBr 10.00

Type C

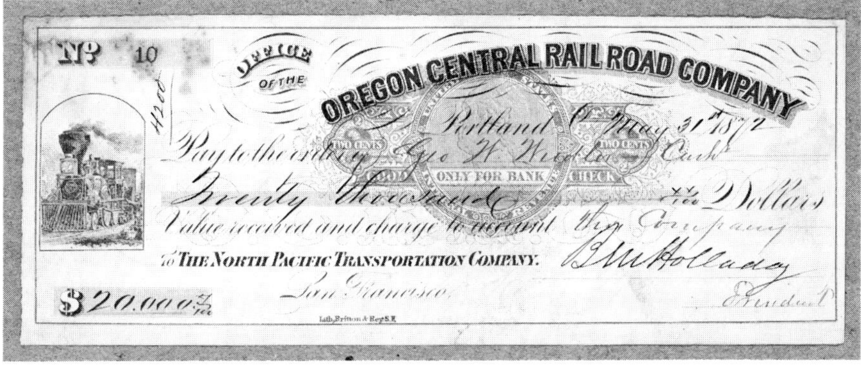

Three part band across lower half of imprint, reading:
GOOD   ONLY FOR BANK   CHECK

C22   Brown   **[RN-C22]**

Drafts
Imprint centered

Portland, Oregon Central Rail Road Co., *red,* B&R 50.00
—, —, same, signature of Ben Holladay 75.00

Type G

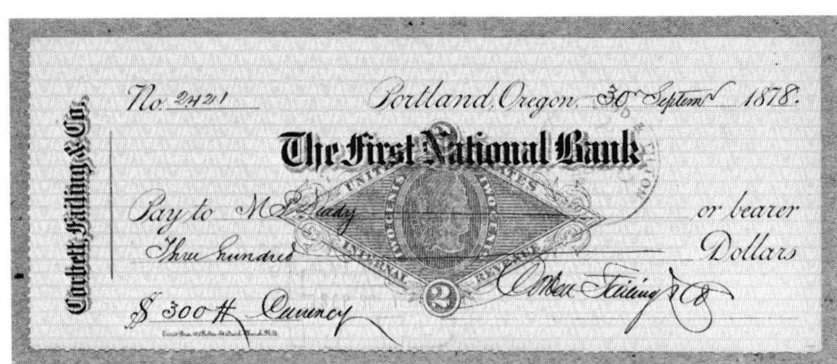

G1　Orange　　　　　　　　　　　　　　　　　　　　**[RN-G1]**

Checks
Imprint centered

Portland, First Nat Bk, *black, orange tint,* EBr 12.00
—, —, Corbett Failing & Co., *black, orange tint,* EBr 10.00

Type X

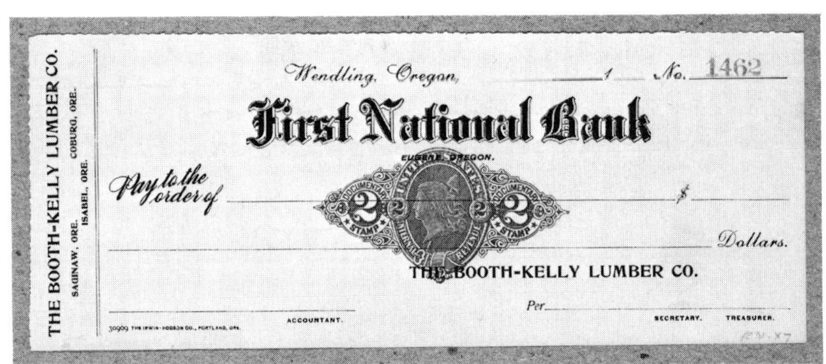

X7　Orange　　　　　　　　　　　　　　　　　　　　**[RN-X7]**

Checks
Imprint centered

Ashland, Bk of Ashland, *green,* ULC 10.00
Baker City, First Nat Bk, IHC 10.00
The Dalles, French & Co., Bankers, CCr 10.00
Oregon City, Bk of Oregon City, IHC 10.00
Wendling, First Nat Bk of Eugene,
　　Booth-Kelly Lumber Co., IHC 10.00

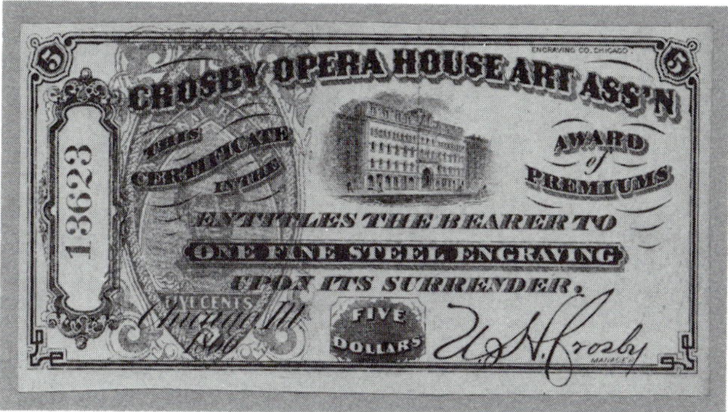

U.S. REVENUES, TAX PAIDS, MATCH & MEDICINE, STATE REVENUES, DOCUMENTS, CANCELS, ETC. BOUGHT & SOLD.

Box 117
Osprey, Florida 34229
Phone (813) 966-5563

Service, Courtesy, Confidence

PTS
LONDON

ASDA
NEW YORK

Utah

Type B

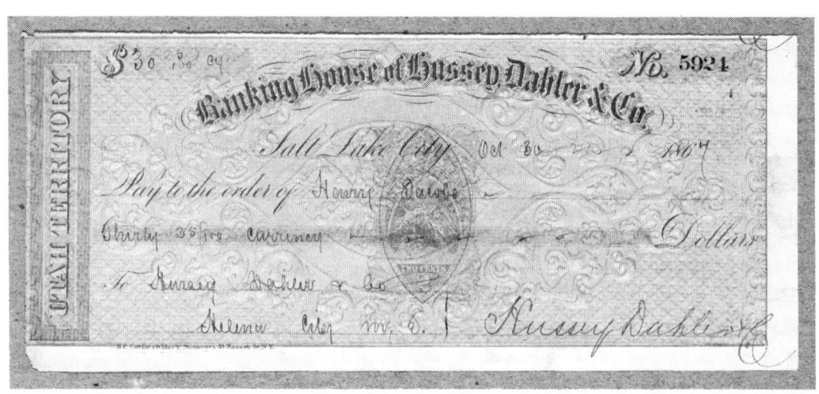

B1   Orange   [RN-B1]

Drafts
Imprint centered

Salt Lake City, Hussey, Dahler & Co., *green, yellow tint,* CMC 40.00

Printed on both sides

B1A   Orange   [RN-B1a]

Receipts
Imprints centered
Receipt size

Salt Lake City, Wells, Fargo & Co., ...   100.00

Type C

C1   Orange   [RN-C1]

Drafts
Imprint centered

Salt Lake City, Walker Bros, *red,* GWC 40.00

Three part band across lower half of imprint, reading:

GOOD   ONLY FOR BANK   CHECK

C21   Orange   **[RN-C21]**

Checks
Imprint centered

Salt Lake City, A.W. White & Co., ... 20.00

Type D

D1   Orange   **[RN-D1]**

Checks
Imprint centered

Salt Lake City, First Nat Bk of Utah, CMC....................... 20.00

Type G

G1   Orange   **[RN-G1]**

Checks
Imprint centered

Ogden, J.E. Dooly & Co., *blue, pink tint, (tan),* WmM 15.00
—, Guthrie, Dooley & Co., *black, pink tint,* AGC 15.00
Park City, Park City Bk, D.C. McLaughlin, *(cream),* WmM 20.00
Salt Lake City, T.R. Jones & Co., *black, gray tint,* ORL. 15.00
—, McCornick & Co., *brown, gray tint,* CMC. 15.00
—, Wells Fargo & Co's Bk, Bac 20.00
Shauntie, Walker Brothers, *(light brown),* BDB 20.00

Type X

X7   Orange   **[RN-X7]**

Checks
Imprint centered

Salt Lake City, Utah Commercial and Savings Bk, *(blue),* CWP 10.00
—, —, Grand Gulch Mining Co., WoT. 12.00
—, Wells Fargo & Co., Bk, Hal. 12.00
—, —, J. Alt, *(yellow),* Hal. 10.00

EMPIRE GROUP
INCORPORATED

PHILIP T. BANSNER   WILLIAM T. CROWE
ALBERT F. CHANG

Exceptional
United States Philately
in all Major Areas

ATTENDANCE AT MOST MAJOR
PHILATELIC EVENTS

* U.S. Classics
* Early Postal History
* 20th Century to 1930
* Revenues
* Proofs & Essays
* Back of the Book

* Possessions

* Auction Agents
* Net Price Sales

SEND NAME AND ADDRESS FOR FREE PRICE LIST

P.O. BOX 2529   WEST LAWN, PA. 19609

TELEPHONE (215) 678-5000

Type X

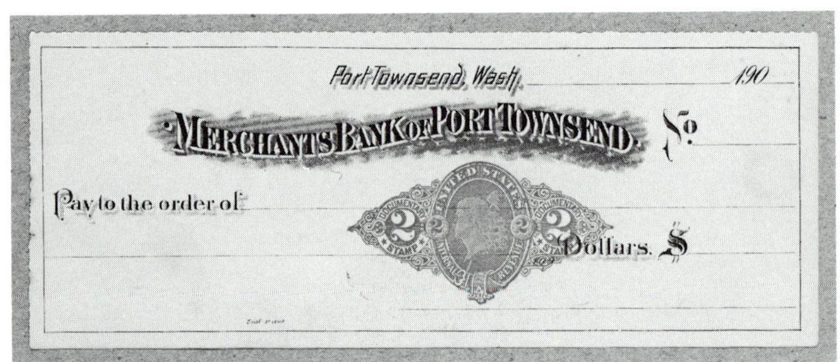

X7   Orange   [RN-X7]

Checks
Imprint centered

Fairhaven, Citizens Nat Bk, ULC	10.00
New Whatcom, Graves & Backus, *(pink)*, Bla	10.00
—, Graves, Backus & Purdy, *(pink)*, Bla	10.00
Port Townsend, Merchants Bk of Port Townsend, *(yellow)*, Gas	12.00
Seattle, Nat Bk of Commerce, *(yellow)*	12.00
Spokane, Exchange Nat Bk, Hal	12.00
Tacoma, Metropolitan Bk, *black, orange tint,* ULC	10.00
—, London & San Francisco Bk, Eric Edw. Rosling, *pink tint,* Bla	12.00

Drafts
Imprint centered

Seattle, Ira Bronson	15.00

Wyoming

Type B

B1   Orange   **[RN-B1]**

Drafts
Imprint centered

Cheyenne, Posey S. Wilson, NBN 75.00

Type G

G1   Orange   **[RN-G1]**

Checks
Imprint centered

Fort Bridger (ms changed from Omaha),
First Nat Bk of Omaha, W.A. Carter, CCo 100.00

Type X

X7   Orange   [RN-X7]

Checks

Imprint centered

Cheyenne, Stock Growers Nat Bk of Cheyenne, *(light green)*, MCJ..	15.00
—, —, *(light brown)*, MCJ	15.00
Laramie, First Nat Bk, *black, gray tint, (gray)*, AGC	25.00

Drafts

Imprint centered

Cheyenne, J.A. Riner, *(yellow)*, PSC	15.00

Type C

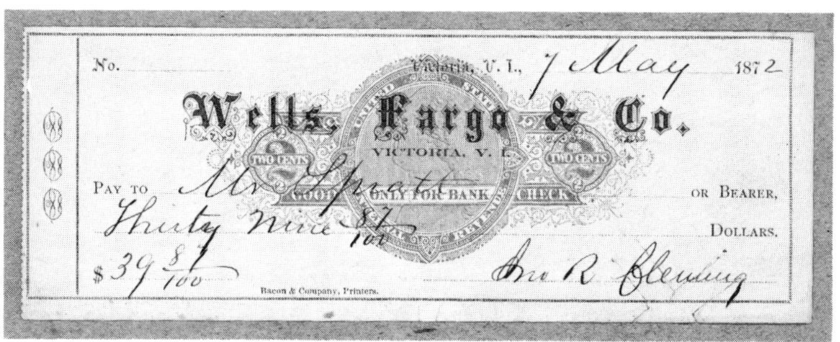

Three part band across lower half of imprint, reading:

GOOD   **ONLY FOR BANK**   **CHECK**

C21   **Orange**   **[RN-C21]**

Checks
Imprint centered

Victoria, Wells, Fargo & Co., Bac. 100.00

Type X

X7   **Orange**   **[RN-X7]**

Checks
Imprint centered

Batopilas, Alexander R. Shepherd,
  (an additional 2¢ 'battleship' revenue added) 100.00

ADDITIONAL ENTRIES

STATE	TYPE	CITY		BANK			
USER			COLOR		PRINTER		★ ⊙

STATE	TYPE	CITY		BANK			
USER			COLOR		PRINTER		★ ⊙

STATE	TYPE	CITY		BANK			
USER			COLOR		PRINTER		★ ⊙

STATE	TYPE	CITY		BANK			
USER			COLOR		PRINTER		★ ⊙

STATE	TYPE	CITY		BANK			
USER			COLOR		PRINTER		★ ⊙

STATE	TYPE	CITY		BANK			
USER			COLOR		PRINTER		★ ⊙

LIST OF PRINTERS

The following is a list of the three-letter designations used within the catalog and the full names of the printers as they appear on the documents. Minor variations in the names are to be expected. However if the variations are substantial, or possibly represent a different firm or a change in the firm's principals, a separate listing has been made.

A&A	Alpaugh & Anderson, Trenton, NJ		Bra	Brandon Printing Co., Nashville, TN
A&B	Arthur & Bonnell, NY		BrB	Brower Bros, NY
A&C	Anderson and Cameron, NY		Bre	Brett Litho. Co., NY
A&K	Affleck & Knapp, NY		BuK	Bugbee & Kelly, Providence
A&P	Averett & Peckett, NY		C&A	Collins & Allen, New Bedford, MA
A&T	Alpaugh & Thompson, Trenton, NJ		C&B	Collins & Brother, NY
A&V	Ashby & Vincent, Erie, PA		C&C	Cushing & Cave, Galveston, TX
AAM	Andrew A. Moser		C&H	Christian & Hyatt, New Orleans
ABN	American Bank Note Co., NY (and Boston)		C&J	Cornwell & Johnson, NY
ABr	A. Brown, NY		C&R	Clay & Richmond, Buffalo, NY
ACH	A.C. Harrison, NY		C&S	Chambers & Sons, London, England
AGC	A. Gast & Co., St. Louis		C&T	Croker & Telfer, NY
AHC	A. Hoen & Co., Baltimore (and Richmond, VA)		C&W	Cross--- & West, Phila.
			CAB	C.A. Bonesteel & Co.
AJL	A.J. Leary, San Francisco		CBC	Cushing, Bardua & Co., NY
ALB	A.L. Bancroft & Co., San Francisco (same as Ban)		CBN	Continental Banknote Co., NY
			CBV	Cornwell Bros. & Vogler, NY
AMC	Andr. M'Chain & Co., Ithaca, NY		CCa	Chapman & Carter, Providence
AML	Andrus, McChain & Lyons (Ithaca, NY)		CCB	Cosack & Co., Buffalo, NY
AmP	American Print, Media, PA		CCC	Clay, Cosack & Co., Buffalo, NY
APC	American Phototype Co., NY		CCo	Chas. M. Cornwell, NY
APE	Art Printing Establishment, NY		CCr	C.H. Crocker, Portland, OR
ArB	Arthur Brown, NY		CCW	Cunningham, Curtiss & Welch, San Francisco
ARG	Aaron R. Gay & Co., Boston			
Arm	Armstrong, Printer, Selma, AL		CFK	Chas. F. Ketcham, NY
Art	Arthur & Co., NY		CGC	C.G. Crawford & Co., NY
ASB	A.S. Baynes, NY		Cha	Chandler, Printer
B&B	Braden & Burford		CHC	Charles H. Clayton & Co., NY
B&C	Bowne & Co., NY		Chi	Chicago Lithographing Co.
B&D	Bingham & Dodd, Hartford, CT		Chu	Thos. Chubbuck
B&G	Bradley & Gilbert, Print		CHy	C. Hyllested, NY
B&H	Bugbee & Hall, Providence		CJD	C.J. Duxbury, Phila.
B&J	Baldwin & Jones, NY		Cla	Clarks, (Phila.)
B&K	Breuker & Kessler, Phila.		CLB	Case, Lockwood & Brainard, Hartford, CT
B&M	Bird & Mickle, Jackson, MI		CLC	The Calvert Lith. Co., Detroit
B&O	Bodine & Odell, NY		Clk	Clark & Courts Lith, Galveston
B&P	Brown & Power, San Francisco		CIS	E.B. Clayton's Sons
B&R	Britton & Rey, San Francisco		Cly	Clay & Co., Buffalo, NY
B&S	Beatty & Stevenson, NY		CMC	Corlies, Macy & Co., NY
B&T	Bugbee & Thompson, Providence		COC	Cooper, Olcott & Co., Savannah, GA
B&W	Brown & Warner, NY		COJ	C.O. Jones, NY
Bac	Bacon & Co., San Francisco		Col	Collier & Cleaveland, Denver
BaK	Baker & Kennedy, Phila.		Com	Commercial Print, Toledo
Ban	Bancroft, San Francisco (same as ALB)		Coo	Cooke & Cobb, NY
BaR	Bannon & Ramsey, Pottsville, PA		Cor	Cortland Standard and Journal Steam Printing House
BBa	B.D. Bacon, NY			
BDB	Benj. D. Benson, NY		CoS	Collins & Sesnon, NY
BDC	Bingham, Dodd & Co., Hartford, CT		Cou	Courier Co., Buffalo, NY
Ben	Benedicks & Sulzbacker, NY		Cow	Cowan & Co., NY
BEP	Bosqui Eng. & P'T'G Co., San Francisco		CPC	Curtis Printing Co., St. Paul
BES	B. Earl & Son, Fall River, NY		CPH	Culver, Page & Hoyne, Chicago
BFS	B.F. Sterett, San Francisco (same as Ste)		CSC	Chas. Shober & Co., Chicago Lithographing Com, Chicago
BHC	B.H. Cappe, NY			
Bla	Blatchly & Co., Tacoma, WA		CSP	Courier Steam Print
Blo	Bloch & Co.		CSS	Chas. S. Stone, Denver
BNH	B.N. Hurd, Titusville, PA		CrC	Crocker & Co., NY
BPK	Brown, Pettibone & Kelly, Chicago		Cri	Crichton & Co., NY

Cro	Crocker & Co's Print., San Francisco, (also Sacramento)
CTC	Cutter, Tower & Co., Boston
Cus	Cushings & Bailey, Baltimore
CWB	Clark W. Bryan, Springfield, MA
CWP	C.W. Pomeroy, Chicago
D&A	Day & Ackerman, NY
D&B	Dennison & Brown, NY
D&C	Democrat and Chronicle Print
D&G	Doane & Greenough, (Boston)
D&S	Dennison & Smith (or Dennison, Smith & Co.), NY
DAC	D. Appleton & Co., NY
DBH	Dean Bros. & Hoffmann, Chicago
DBr	Dean Bros., Chicago
DCG	De Witt C. Gardner, NY
Dea	M.C. Dean, Chicago
DFS	Daily Freeman Steam Print, Kingston, NY
Dix	C.A. Dixon, (Phila)
DLC	Denver Litho Co., Denver
DLP	D.L. Proudfit, NY
DoB	Donaldson Brothers, Five Points, NY
Dor	Dore & Co., San Francisco
Dou	Douglas, New Orleans
DPC	Dorsey Ptg Co., Dallas
DTP	Dorat the Printer
DVA	D.L. Van Antwerp, Albany, NY
E&K	Ehrgott & Krebs, Cincinnati
E&S	Ester & Smith, NY
EAC	Ezra A. Cook & Co., Chicago
EAK	E.A. Kingsland & Co., NY
EAL	E.A. Lewis & Co., Bridgeport, CT
Ear	B. Earl & Sons, Fall River, MS (MA?)
EBC	Edward Bosqui & Co., (also Bosqui & Co., San Francisco)
EBr	Everit Bros., NY
ECP	Evening Chronicle Print
ECr	Eugene D. Croker, NY
EDC	Edward Denny & Co., San Francisco
EdM	Ed. Mandel, Chicago
EDS	E.D. Slater, NY
EFB	E.F. Brainard & Co., NY
EFC	Ehrgott, Forbriger & Co., Cincinnati
Egb	Egbert, Fidler & Chambers, Davenport, IA
EJH	E.J. Hale & Son, NY
EJK	Edwin J. Kerr & Co., NY
ENG	E.N. Grattan, Phila.
EPH	Eagle Printing House
ESD	E.S. Dodge & Co., NY
ESt	Edward Stern, Phila.
ERS	E.R. Stevens, Saratoga Springs, NY
EWS	E. Wells Sackett & Bro., NY
F&A	Forst & Averell, NY
F&V	Francis & Valentine
FAT	F.A. Trafton, NY
FBo	F. Boegle. Print
FCP	F.C. Philbrick & Co., Boston
FFN	Frank F. Newland, NY
FFT	F.F. Taylor, NY
FHC	F. Heppenheimer & Co., NY
FLF	F.L. Fischer
FMI	F.M. Ives, Chicago
FMS	Ferd Mayer & Sons, NY
Fos	F. Foster, (Phila.)
FSc	F. Scofield, Phila.
FSH	F.S. Hickman, West Chester, PA
Fra	Frank & Co., San Francisco

G&B	German & Bro., Louisville
G&C	German & Co., NY
G&D	Gluyas & Dutton, San Francisco
G&G	John A. Gray & Green, NY
G&M	Grogan & Murtha, NY
G&W	Guggenheimer & Weil, Baltimore
Gal	Galloway Litho. Co., San Francisco
Gas	Gast, St. Louis (same as AGC)
Gav	Gavit & Co., Albany, NY
GBL	Geo. B. Lockwood, NY
GBr	Gifford Bros., NY
GDB	Geo. D. Barnard, St. Louis, MO
GFN	George F. Nesbitt & Co., NY
GHD	George H. Denny & Co., St. Louis
GHW	Geo. H. Whitney
Gib	Gibson & Co., Cincinnati
Gie	Gies & Co., Buffalo, NY
GlB	Gladding Brothers & Co., Providence
GNN	Geo. N. Nichols, Savannah, GA
Gor	Gorman & Co., NY
GrB	Griffith & Byrne, NY
GRC	G. Rayner & Co., Yonkers, NY
GRD	Gresham & Dawson, NY
GTB	G.T. Brown & Co., San Francisco
GTP	Geo. T. Patterson Stationary Co., NY
Gug	H. Gugler & Son, Milwaukee
GWC	Great Western Lithographing Co., Chicago
GWL	G.W. Lewis, Albany, NY
GWP	Geo. W. Pertain, NY
H&A	Hamilton & Adams, NY
H&C	Hatch & Co., NY, (also Hatch Litho Co., NY & Boston)
H&H	Hickman & Hammond, West Chester, PA
H&M	Heppenheimer & Maurer, NY
H&O	Hall & O'Donald Litho Co., Topeka, KS
H&S	Hosford & Sons, NY
Hae	J. Haehnlen, Phila.
Hal	Hall Litho Co., Topeka, KS
Ham	C. Hamilton, St. Louis
HaP	Harrison Printers, San Francisco
Har	Harnersley & Co.
Has	Hastings & Habberton, NY
HBr	Hetsch Bros., Newport, KY
HCK	H.C. Kessler, Butte, MT
HCS	H.C. Stoothoff, NY
HDJ	Henry Dawson Jr., NY
HHu	H. Hutchinson & Co., Phila.
HLC	Hooper, Lewis & Co., Boston
HLD	Hall L. Davis, Portland, ME
HLG	Helfenstein, Lewis & Green, Phila.
HNC	H. Niedecken & Co., Milwaukee
Hob	Samual Hobbs & Co., Boston
HoC	Hollowbush & Carey, Phila.
HoH	Horace Holden, NY
HPC	Hannibal Printing Co., Hannibal, MO
HPH	Hutchings Printing House, Hartford, CT
HPL	H.P. Lawry, NY
HRC	H.R. Cooper, NY
HRH	Hugh R. Hildreth Printing Co., St. Louis
HSB	Henry Seibert & Bros., NY
HSC	H.S. Crocker & Co., San Francisco
HSp	Henry Spear, NY
I&M	Ives & Marshall, Chicago
I&W	Ives & Walstrom, (Phila.)
ICT	Isaac C. Titus, NY
IHC	Irwin Hodson Co., Portland, OR
IJP	Ithaca Journal Print

J&C	Jordan & Co., NY
J&S	Johnson & Smith, Minneapolis
JAL	John A. Lowell & Co.
JBC	J.B. Chandler, Phila.
JBi	J. Bien, NY
JBL	J.B. Lippincott & Co., Phila.
JCC	John C. Clark & Son, Phila.
JCF	James C. Filor & co., NY
JCH	J.C. Hall, Providence
HCL	J.C. Lutz & Co., Springfield, (MA)
JDy	Johnson-Dyer (artist, rather than printer?)
JFS	F.F. Saunders & Co., Cincinnati
JGH	John G. Hodge & Co., San Francisco
JGi	John Gibson, NY, (also J. Gibson)
JHa	John Hamilton, NY
JHD	J.H. Duyckinch, NY
JHW	J.H. Warner, NY
JJB	J.J. Bloomfield, NY
JLK	J.L. Kervand
JLM	John L. Murphy, Trenton, NJ
JoP	Johnston's Print
Jor	Jordan Stationary Co., NY (probably same as J&C)
JOS	J.O. Seymour & Co., NY
Jou	Journal Print, Kingston, NY
JMB	John M. Burnet
JME	J.M. Ensminger, Manheim, PA
JMF	J. Milton Ferry, NY
JMW	J.M. Whittemore & Co., Boston
JMJ	J.M.W. Jones, Chicago
JPM	John P. Morton & Co. (C19)
JRM	J.R. Mills & Co.
JSC	James Sutton & Co., NY
JSH	John S. Hulin & Co., NY
JWB	J.W. Burke & Co., Macon, GA
JWG	J. West Goodwin, Sedalia, MO
JWM	J.W. Middleton, Chicago
JWS	J.W. Steel, Phila.
K&B	Kellogg & Bulkeley, Hartford, CT
K&C	J. Knauber & Co., Milwaukee
K&H	Kennard & Hay, NY
K&T	Kores & Toby, NY
KDF	Kingston Daily Freeman, Kingston, NY
Ket	E. Ketterlinus, Phila.
KNP	King, Newland & Proudfit, NY
Kor	Korff Brothers, NY
Kre	Krebs Lithographing Co., Cincinatti
L&B	Levison & Blythe, St. Louis
L&C	Longacre & Co.
LAL	Los Angeles Litho Co., Los Angeles
LBB	L.B. Brooks
LBC	Levey Bros & Co., Indianapolis
LBr	LeCount Bros., San Francisco
LeB	Lehman & Bolton, Phila.
LeC	LeCount & Mansur, San Francisco
Lev	Levey Bros. & Co., Indianapolis
LFL	L.F. Lawrence, Boston
LHB	L.H. Biglow & Co., NY
Lou	Louisville Lithographing Co.
LPH	The Leiseuring Printing House, Phila.
LSc	Louis Schwarz
LSL	Louisville Steam Lith. Co.
LuB	Lucas Bros., Baltimore
M&B	Murphy & Bechtel, Trenton, NJ
M&C	Moss & Co., Phila.
M&E	Mohun & Ebbs, NY
M&H	Macoy & Herwig, NY

M&K	Major & Knapp Eng., Mfg. & Lith. Co., NY
M&M	Mayer & Merkel, NY
M&S	E.C. Markley & Son, Phila.
M&W	Maverick & Wissinger, NY
Mac	MacGowan & Slipper, NY
Mad	J.W. Madden, New Orleans
Mal	Robt. Malcolm, NY
MAM	Munroe & Metz, NY
Man	Mann, Steam-Power Printer (probably same as WmM)
MaS	Marvin & Son, Pr., (Boston)
Max	Maxwell & Co., Louisville
MBC	Milton Bradley & Co., Springfield, MA
McD	McDonald Bros. & Dillont, NY
McI	McIlwain & Brooks, Phila.
MCJ	Milton C. Johnson, NY
McK	J. McKittrick & Co., St. Louis
McL	McLaughlin Brothers
McM	W. McMurray, (Phila.)
McN	McNutt, Kahn & Co, San Francisco
MCo	Melhado & Cooper, NY
McS	McLean, Sherwood & Co., NY
MEl	Miller & Elder, Phila.
Mer	Merchants Litho Co., Chicago
Mil	Mills & Co., Des Moines, IA
MLE	Milwaukee Litho. & Engr. Co., Milwaukee
MLL	Mutual Label & Lith Co., San Francisco
MMO	Meyer, Merkel & Ottmann, NY
Mor	Robert Morton, NY
MRW	M.R. Warren & Co., Boston
MSC	Maverick, Stephan & Co., NY
Mun	F. Munson, Chicago
N&P	Newland & Proudfit, NY
NaL	Nathan Lane, NY
NBN	National Bank Note Co., NY
NEB	New England Bank Note Co., Boston
Nes	Nesbitt & Co.
NLS	Nathan Lane's Sons, NY
NNW	New North-West Lithograph Agency
NYE	New York Economical Printing Co., NY
NYL	N.Y. Lithg, Engg & Printing Co., (probably same as NYP)
NYP	NY Printing Co., NY
Out	Outwest Printing & Stationary Co., Colorado Springs
O&S	Osford & Sons, NY
ORL	Omaha Republican Lith. & Printers
OtK	Otto Krebs, Pittsburgh
P&B	Pease & Booth, NY
P&C	Pelletreau & Cole, NY
P&G	Punderson & Grisand, New Haven, CT
P&R	Pelletreau & Raynor, NY
P&S	Proudfit & Stone, NY
P&T	Pease & Titus, NY
PDu	Paulin Durel, New Orleans
PEB	Philip E. Bogert, NY
Pio	Pioneer Press, St. Paul
PJC	Price, Jones & Co., Memphis, TN
PLC	Phoenix Lith Co., Buffalo & Chicago
Por	J.B. Porter, Wilmington, DE
PSC	Pettibone, Sawtell & Co., Chicago
PUC	Payot, Upham & Co., San Francisco
Pue	Pueblo Litho Co.
Q&F	Quinan & Frost, NY
R&A	Geo. C. Rand and Avery, Boston, (also Rand, Avery & Co.)

R&B	Richmonds & Backus, Detroit, (also Richmond, Backus & Co.)
R&T	Reen & Trump, Phila.
RAC	R.C. Root, Anthony & Co., NY
RAF	Rand, Avery & Frye, Boston
Ray	G. Rayner & Co., Yonkers, NY
RBT	R.B. Taber, New Bedford, (MA)
Reg	Register, Bordentown, NJ
ReL	Republican Lith, Omaha, NB
Rep	Republican Print, West Chester, PA
Rev	Review Printer, Phila.
RFM	R.F. Macoy, NY
RGH	R.G. Hutchinson, NY
RMc	Rand, McNally & Co., Chicago
Rob	Martin Roberts. NY
Roe	T.W. Roe & Co., NY
RPB	Republican Print, Binghampton, NY
RPS	R.P. Studley Co., St. Louis
RWH	Rawdon, Wright, Hatch & Edson, NY
S&A	Steele & Avery, Rochester, NY
S&B	Stearns & Beale, NY
S&C	Strobridge & Co., Cincinnati
S&H	Sanford & Hayward, Cleveland, OH
S&J	Slote & Janes, NY
S&K	Simons & Keiningham
S&L	Seifert & Lawton, Milwaukee
S&M	Saxton & Morton, NY
S&P	Steng & Paxson, Phila.
SaC	Sanford & Co., Cleveland, OH
San	Sanford & Co., Worchester, MA
SBC	Sutton, Bowne & Co., NY
SBe	S. Benedicks & Co., NY
SBl	Snyder & Black, NY
SBS	Snyder, Black & Sturn, NY
SCC	Sanford, Cushing & Co., Boston
SCl	Strickland & Clarke, Galveston, TX
Sco	C. Scott, Trenton, NJ
SCT	S.C. Toof & Co., Memphis, TN
Scu	Scudder's Print
SDA	S.D. Affleck, NY
Sed	Sedalia Bazoo Print
Sha	Sharp, Printer, Trenton, NJ
ShC	Shober & Carqueville Lith Co., Chicago
SHW	Stewart, Haring & Warren, NY
Sid	Siddall Prothers, (Phila.)
SJP	State Journal Print, Jefferson City, MO
SKH	J.O. Seymour, Kennard & Hay, NY
SLa	Sargent & Lawrence, Boston
SLB	St. Louis Book & News Co.
SLC	South. Lith Co., Richmond, VA
SLE	Stephens Litho & Eng. Co., St. Louis
SLL	Salt Lake Litho Co.
SMN	Savannah Morning News Print
Spy	Spy, Steam Job Print
SSC	Sage, Sons & Co., Buffalo, NY
SSM	S.S. Motley, NY
SRJ	S.R. Johnston & Co.
Ste	Sterett, Printer
StJ	St. Joseph Steam Printing Co.
StL	St. Louis Bank Note Co.
StP	St. Paul Press
Str	B.S. Stradley, NY
SWC	Samuel Ward & Co., Boston
T&C	Thalmessinger & Cahn, NY
T&F	F.F. Taylor & Francis, NY
T&H	Taylor & Hickman, West Chester, PA
T&J	Thayer & Jackson Stationary Co., Chicago
T&R	Tibbitts & Randall, Providence
T&S	Tibbits & Shaw, Providence
TCC	Toppan, Carpenter & Co., Cincinatti
TDC	Terrell, Dietz & Co., Louisville
TFC	T. Fitzwilliam & Co., New Orleans
TGC	Thomas Groom & Co., Boston
TGi	Tower, Bildersleeve & Co., NY
Tha	M. Thalmessinger, NY
ThL	Theo. Leonhardt, Phila.
Ths	T.H. Saunders, London, England
TMT	Tuttle, Morehouse & Taylor, Print.
Tom	K. Tompins, NY
Tre	Tremain & Co., NY
Tri	Tribune Co.
Tun	Tunis, Detroit
Tut	Tuttle & Co., Rutland, VT
TWP	Thos. W. Price Co., Phila.
UBN	Union Bank Note Co., Kansas City, MO
ULC	Union Litho Co., San Francisco
UtL	Utah Litho Co., Salt Lake City
VAC	Valpey, Angell & Co., Providence
VBW	Videl, Brown & Warner, NY
Veg	Ed A. Veghte, Somerville, N.J
VKC	Van Kleeck, Clark & Co., NY
VMR	V.M. Ramee, NY
W&B	White & Brayton, Buffalo & Chicago
W&C	Waters & Co., San Francisco
W&H	Wilbur & Hastings, NY
W&K	Wemple & Kronheim & Co., NY
W&P	Williams & Plum, Newark, NJ
W&R	Wm. H. Woglom & Reading, NY
W&T	Wright & Towers, NY
W&Z	Waldheimer & Zenn, NY
WAS	Wm. A. Speaight & Co., NY
WAW	William A. Wheeler, NY
WBB	Wm. B. Burford, Indianapolis
WBC	Wilstack, Baldwin & Co., Cincinnati
WBD	W.B. Dickie, NY
WBN	Western Bank Note & Engraving Co., Chicago
WCH	Wm. C. Hutchings, Hartford, CT
WDR	Wm. D. Roe, NY
WEC	Western Engraving Co., Chicago (also St. Louis), probably same as WBN
WE&	Walker, Evans & Cogswell
WES	Wm. Everdall's Sons, NY
WFC	Willard Felt & Co., NY
WFM	Wm. F. Murphy's Son's, Phila.
WFR	W.F. Robinson & Co., Denver
WGP	W.G. Perry Stationer, Phila
WHA	W.H. Arthur & Co., NY
WHC	W.H. Crocker, NY
WHi	Wilson Hinkle & Co., Cincinnati
WhP	Wheeler, Phelan & Co., San Francisco
WHW	Wm. H. Woglom, NY
WJM	W.J. Morgan, Cleveland, OH
WMC	Wm. M. Christy, Phila.
WmM	Wm. Mann, Phila.
WMS	Wm. Mann & Sons, NY
WNC	Waters, Newhoff & Co., San Francisco
WoT	Woodward & Tiernan, St. Louis
WPC	Weed, Parsons & Co., Albany, NY
WPH	William P. Harrison, San Francisco
WTN	W.T. Nicholson, Trenton, NJ
WWa	Willy Wallach, NY
WWG	Wm.W. Geer, NY
Zan	Zane, Pr(inter)

A Gleam of Light on a Shady By-Way,
or the Seventh Issue Revenue Stamp on Parlor or Sleeping Car Tickets.

By H. N. Mudge.

The philatelic feature of the subject under consideration is so interwoven with another and entirely foreign feature that it may be questioned whether, in attempting to follow this line of study, one is investigating a detail of the seventh issue of the United States revenue stamps or is studying a phase of railroad tickets. Sure it is, however, that the ticket feature predominates, and yet the ticket has its legitimate philatelic bearing on account of its being the paper, or medium, carrying the stamp, and on account of the treatment of the stamp on various forms of tickets.

The fact of having to deal, in this connection, with a ticket issued by a railroad company, or by an allied transportation company, the two pursuing exactly, or approximately, the same methods as to the issue and use of tickets, makes the matter difficult to follow to a complete conclusion at this late day. During the taxing period of three years and ten months, millions of these tickets were issued with stamps printed on them, but it is doubtful if one hundred of them exist intact today; excepting possibly, a bunch of some one or two issues that some philatelically minded person caused to be switched on to a preservation-side-track at the time they were current. From the moment in their manufacture when they received their numbers to the time of their final destruction in the cutting machine or furnace, they represented a specific money value and were the subject of a strict accounting. Except a portion of some of them, they were never in the hands of the public longer than from the time of their purchase until they were surrendered on the accommodations they represented being furnished. Furthermore, in the majority of the forms issued, at no time did the purchaser hold intact the complete ticket as printed; and, on being issued or used, they were divided into from two to four parts, which parts were distributed in as many different channels. As a final chapter in the life of these stamp-bearing tickets the following extract from a letter to the writer is typical of many such, and will show why the usual last prop of the philatelist, remainders, has been removed in this case:—"We have made a thorough search through our stock room, but find that they have all been destroyed. When the use of these stamps was discontinued, the tickets on hand were sent to Washington to have the stamps redeemed."

From this it will be seen that at all times this matter of a printed revenue stamp on sleeping and parlor car tickets was more or less difficult to approach from a collector's point of view, and that at this late day the subject is more than ever a shady philatelic by-way. It is proposed, therefore, to throw a few rays of light on to the by-way in order that a record may be made of this interesting subject before the foliage of oblivion has grown so dense around it that no rays of light can penetrate the tangle. It is not claimed that the record is final in all details, but it is believed that the following sets forth in a broad way the complete story, with sufficient detail to serve as an ample illustration of any or all possible omissions.

First, as to the law that brought this class of paper within the philatelic list. It was approved June 13th, 1898, was effective from the date mentioned therein until April 12th, 1902, and read as follows:—"That from and after the first day of July, eighteen hundred and ninety-eight, a stamp tax of one cent shall be levied and collected on every seat sold in a palace or parlor car, and on every berth sold in a sleeping car, the stamp to be affixed to the ticket and paid by the company issuing the same." In this it should be noted particularly that the payment of the tax by placing the revenue stamp on the tickets was not a conception of the issuing companies, but was a requirement of the law. For a short time until the Government had provided facilities for the stamp to be printed on the tickets, the tax was paid by attaching adhesive revenue stamps to the tickets and checks as issued. With some railroads this method was employed throughout the taxing period, their sleeping or parlor car business being insufficient to warrant, or for other reasons they not desiring, the special printing of the stamp. Tickets and checks thus treated, being simply one of hundreds of other kinds of documents to which adhesives were attached, have no claim for consideration in connection with this article beyond this statement of fact as a matter of record.

The stamp printed on the parlor and sleeping car ticket was the design furnished by the government in the seventh series for all documents, and so of course was the same as that used on bank checks, except that it was printed in two denominations. Firms in various parts of the country were licensed to print these stamps, and as a rule, such firms were not ticket printers. Hence the tickets were generally printed at one place, after which they were sent to another to have the stamps printed on them, as the licensed printers would not reverse the order of procedure. As a consequence, on all stamped tickets thus handled by two firms, the stamp was printed over the type matter of the tickets.

Tickets with these stamps were printed reading not only from one station to another but each direction between the same stations, and they were also printed for seats in parlor cars, upper berths, lower berths, sleeping car sections, state rooms and drawing rooms; in addition they were printed for a group of stations, the starting and destination points being punched out of a list incorporated in the printed matter of the ticket. Conductor's checks with blanks for writing the stations in when they were issued, and also checks with provision for punching out the stations between which they were issued, were also printed with the stamps on them. These, however, and other differences such as subject matter, should have no philatelic interest except when they altered the character of the tickets and checks and made of them a distinctive document or affected the stamp feature. Such exceptions occur when of two tickets otherwise exactly alike one was for a parlor car

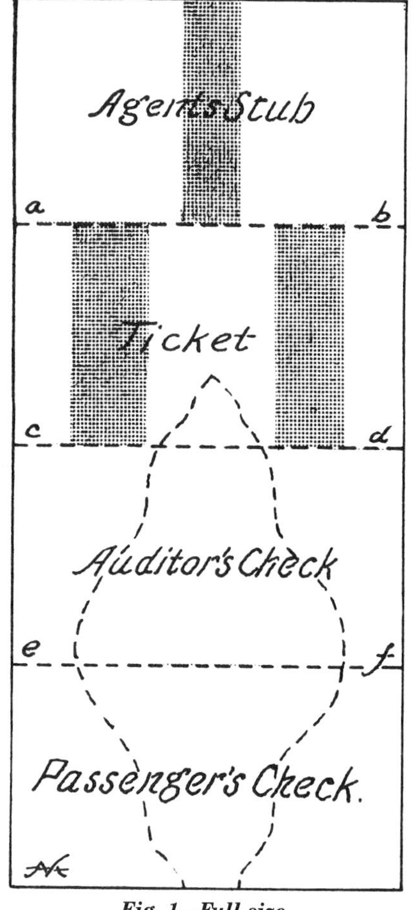

Fig. 1—Full size.

seat and the other for a berth in a sleeping car; in the tickets reading for a section, state room, or drawing room in distinction to the same ticket for a berth or a parlor car seat, as the former, having two berths, had a two cent stamp on them instead of a one cent stamp; and in the structural difference between tickets and between a ticket and a check. Some of these features and the application of the stamp are best brought out by the accompanying diagrams.

In considering them, it should be first understood that one great car company did practically all of the sleeping car and parlor car business during the period under consideration, operating over almost every railroad in the country. In a few exceptional cases, however, individual railroads maintained and operated their own sleeping cars, while more of them operated their own parlor cars. The number of roads operating either, however, was relatively very small, hence a greater part of the story of the revenue stamp on sleeping and parlor car tickets is that told by these of the Pullman Company's issue.

Fig. 1 represents in outline the regular form of ticket of that company as sold by agents. These were of coupon form, being separated by perforation lines, a to f, in four parts, viz; the agent's stub, retained by the selling agent for his record; the ticket proper and the auditor's check, both lifted by the car conductor and the latter, the check, turned over to the porter, each coupon eventually reaching the accounting department; the passenger's check, retained by the passenger as an identification of accommodations. The ticket was printed on white wove paper, and its face, giving points between which it was good, price, nature of accommodations for which it was issued, number and labeling of coupons and other matter, was type printed in black. In addition, the ticket proper, and generally, but not always, the agent's stub, had tinted backgrounds of varying colors and designs. On the back of the ticket proper was the facsimile signature of the General Ticket Agent, and on the back of the passenger's check was the usual notification as to wearing apparel, jewelry, etc.

The revenue stamp was printed *on the back* of this ticket, the long way of the stamp running vertically across the two lower coupons—auditor's and passenger's checks; a bit of the upper end also running in to the third coupon from the bottom. Hence, as will be seen by the illustration, in using this ticket the stamp became severed into about two equal parts, only one of which could be retained by the public. There were occasional variations on this style of ticket in that they were sometimes printed without the agent's stub, and there were so-called special forms of it. The latter generally differed only in being of larger size and in having a list of stations printed on them, the destination of the ticket thus being "station punched." On such a "special" the stamp was generally printed *on the face* of the ticket.

The stamps on the tickets illustrated by Fig. 1 were, broadly speaking, in yellows, green and reds, with various intermediate and combination hues. In fact, the most of them bear evidence of hurried or careless printing in the matter of their color; there being heavy and weak impressions of the same color, and mixtures only to be accounted for by a fresh batch of ink being dumped into an ink fountain from which the ink of another color had not been thoroughly cleaned. The stamps were also in two denominations, according to whether the tickets were for accommodations exceeding a single berth or not. The following varieties have come under the observation of the writer.

On white paper, one cent; on upper and lower berth tickets—pink, carmine, salmon, light red-brown, green; on parlor car seat tickets—carmine, brown-red. On white paper, two cents; one section and state room tickets—yellow, buff, yellow-brown.

Even more interesting perhaps than these tickets, is another form of stamped paper issued by the Pullman Company, and which to the layman generally go by the name of tickets, but which technically are known as conductor's berth, or seat checks. The standard form of this check during the revenue period, is shown in skeleton by Fig. 2. This check was issued in connection with cash payment on trains for sleeping or parlor car accommodations. As is shown, it was divided by a horizontal perforated line into two coupons, the upper coupon being at one time known as the porter's check, and later as the auditor's check, the lower coupon being the passenger's check. They were type printed black on white wove paper, the face of the lower, or passenger's, checks having in addition to their subject matter, an underlying printed color tint. The revenue stamp was printed over all in the center of, and on the face of,

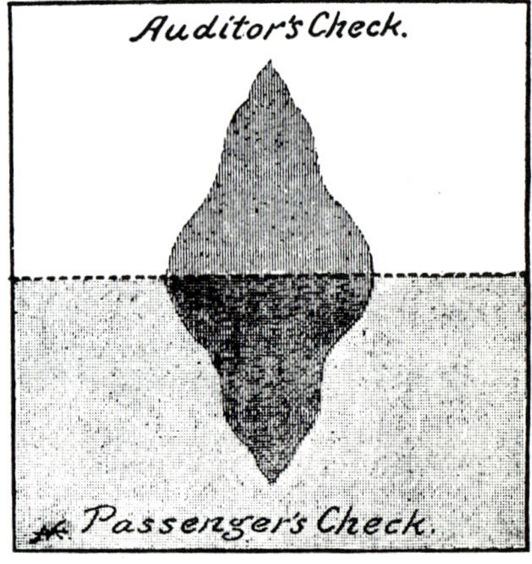

Fig. 2—About three-fifths size.

the check, its long way running vertically across the white and colored coupons in about equal parts. Hence a most interesting and unusual feature occurs in these stamps in that half of them are one color and half another. That is, with the check tint blue and the stamp printed in yellow, the half on the stamp printed in yellow, the half on the tint became olive-green while the half on white showed yellow; again, a stamp printed in pink showed that color on white and lilac over a gray-green tint.

On the back of the passenger's check was the notice as to wearing apparel, etc., and on the face of each check was duplicated matter covering all necessary data pertaining to the sale of accommodations. In issuing, the passenger's and auditor's checks were folded together on the perforated line for the purpose of punching out certain data common to both. They were then separated, one part going to the passenger, which part, it will be noticed, had only one-half of the stamp on it, and that the half modified as to color by being printed over a tint.

The tints were both flat and engraved, and in color were blue, blue-green, gray-green and yellow. The engraved tint consisted of the words "The Pullman Company" cut out from the tint-block in slanting lines, and repeated all over the block in various sizes and directions; open horizontal lines being also incorporated between the groups of lettering. For convenience of future reference this will be designated as "engraved tint C." The stamps, all of which were of one cent denomination, were printed in varying hues of red, yellow and green inks, and of them the following varieties may be listed.

On conductor's berth, or seat, check—standard form, white paper, one cent stamp. Buff on white and over blue flat tint; yellow on white and over blue flat tint; green on white and over blue-green flat tint; pink on white and over gray-green engraved tint C; red on white and over yellow engraved tint C.

In addition to the Pullman regular and special forms of tickets, and the regular form of conductor's check, quite a number of "special" forms of Pullman conductor's check, for use in parlor car service, were issued with the revenue stamp on them, and differed from the standard form in one or all of three broad particulars. They had printed on them a list of stations, the points between which they were good being punched out— this in distinction to the standard form, on which these points were written in. They were larger, and generally, (although not always) of a different shape in that, instead of the two parts being one above another, they were side by side as illustrated by Fig. 3; the passenger's check of these "specials" was sometimes the right, sometimes the left and sometimes the bottom half. The underlying tint on the face of the check as a rule (although again, not always, covered both the passenger's and auditor's checks; there being a separate tint block for each, as shown by Fig. 3. There were three designs used on these tint blocks, viz.: engraved tint A, monogram "P. P. C. Co" in double open line letters in center of open line lathe work; engraved tint B, solid open letters in three slanting lines, the lines reading "The Pullman Co" and being in the center of an

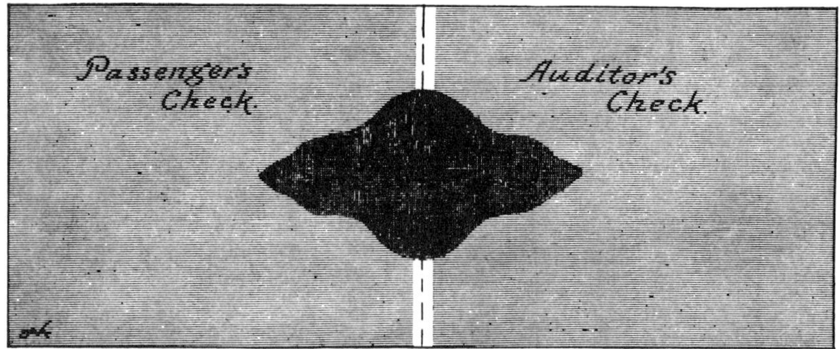

Fig. 3—About three-fifths size.

otherwise plain tint; engraved tint C, being, as previously described, the words "The Pullman Company" cut out from the tint-block in slanting lines, and repeated all over the block in various sizes and directions, open horizontal lines being also incorporated between the groups of lettering. The following varieties of the printed revenue stamp on these special forms of conductor's seat checks is, it is believed, fairly illustrative of this additional feature of the subject under consideration.

All checks printed on white paper, and all stamps of one cent denomination. Yellow stamp, printed horizontally across center and over light bluish-green engraved tint "A" on passenger's (left half) check—auditor's check (right half) probably the same. Orange stamp, printed horizontally across center over light lemon-yellow engraved tint "A" on passenger's (left half) check—auditor's check (right half) probably the same. Yellow-brown stamp, printed horizontally across center over gray-brown engraved tints "A" on both passenger's and auditor's checks—passenger's check to the right. Green stamp, printed horizontally across center over yellow engraved tint block "B", on passenger's (left half) check—auditor's check (right half) probably the same. Carmine stamp, printed vertically across center over yellow-green engraved tint "C" on lower (passenger's) check, and on white upper (auditor's) check, this last half not being tinted.

The railroad's story of the use of a printed revenue stamp is quickly told. Of the hundreds of roads over which, during the Spanish War period, one might ride in a sleeping or parlor car, twenty-three is about, if not exactly, the number of them that ran sleeping or parlor cars of their own. Of this twenty-three about a third of them paid the tax on seats and berths by the use of an adhesive stamp. Of the remainder, the following is illustrative of probably all that is of interest in the matter from a philatelic point of view.

One of the large western roads printed the stamp on practically the same forms of regular ticket and conductor's train check as have been described for the Pullman Company; and a road in the south-east used the same form of conductor's berth check with a stamp printed thereon. A northern road, that for both its sleeping and parlor cars used adhesives for tickets sold at stations, printed a stamp on the conductor's seat check used on parlor cars, which check is the simplest in form of all that have come under the writer's observation. It is illustrated by Fig. 4; and of it it is only necessary to say that it was issued by the train conductor at the time of payment for accommodations by the passenger, and was taken up by the porter.

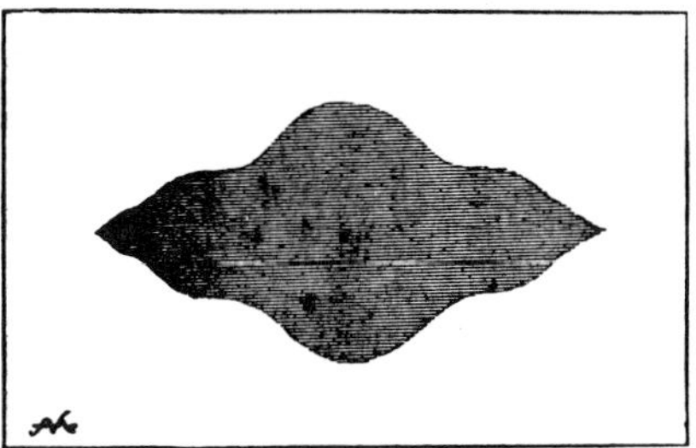

Fig. 4—Little over half size.

Another large western road, that rans its own parlor cars, print.ed the stamp on four forms of parlor car tickets, namely: on so-called ordinary card tickets, on a conductor's check, on local simplex tickets and on interline simplex ticket. Fig. 5 illustrates the interline simplex ticket, it being understood that the word interline in this connection refers to a ticket that is issued for use over two or more distinct railroads. The ordinary simplex ticket mentioned as having also been issued with stamp, was similar to the part of Fig. 5 above the line x. y., and was for use on one, the issuing, road only.

The interline ticket shown in skeleton by the figure, is interesting in that, like other tickets that have been described, in their use they were so divided and separated as to practically prohibit the philatelist from acquiring the complete document that carried the revenue stamp. And, worse yet, no part of the ticket was ever retained by the passenger, thus depriving him of a chance of even half a stamp, as in the case of the Pullman tickets.

The ticket as printed, note Fig. 5, was in one piece, and had a triplicate list of stations printed on it as shown by the figures and lines 1 to 11. It was perforated at the line x. y.; the portion below that line being the ticket of the initial, or selling road; the portion above the line being that of the terminal road, and also containing the auditor's stub, the latter being retained by the selling road. On the lower and on

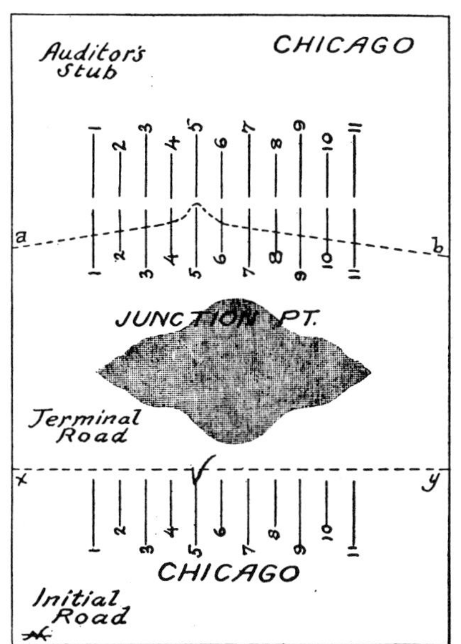

Fig. 5—Little less than half size.

the auditor's portions was printed the name of the station from which the ticket was sold; it will also be noted that the lists of stations 1 to 11 were on each of the three parts that have been described. On the lower part of the terminal road ticket was printed the name of the junction point of the two railroads at interest in the issue of the ticket; also the revenue stamp.

Suppose now, the ticket was sold for a parlor car seat from Chicago to station 5. The selling agent, in issuing the ticket checked off with a pen station 5 on the lower, or initial road's portion, and with a simplex cutter separated, as shown by the line a. b., the top of the ticket in a manner to show on both portions the destination, or station 5. The auditor's stub went to the initial road; the conductor of the initial road tore off and lifted the portion below x.y., and which was good from Chicago to the junction point, and the conductor of the terminal, or second, road lifted the remainder, or portion between a.b. and x.y., that was good from the junction point to destination. Thus it will be seen that two portions of the document went in one direction, while the third, with the stamp on it, went in another.

The revenue stamps printed by railroad companies in connection with the tickets thus outlined, may be incompletely listed as follows: yellow paper, parlor car check, one cent green and yellow-green stamp on face. White paper, conductor's berth check, one cent yellow stamp on face, half on white and half over green flat tint. White paper, conductor's sleeping and parlor car check, one cent green stamp on face, half on white and half over yellow-green horizontal wavy-line engraved tint. Yellow-coated paper (white on reverse side) simplex interline parlor car ticket, one cent buff stamp on face, the yellow coated side.

Such is the story of the revenue stamp on parlor and sleeping car tickets that commemorate the Spanish War. It has been told thus imperfectly to rescue it from oblivion—before it fades from a shady philatelic by-way to one of obliterating darkness.

The above description of revenue stamped railroad tickets appeared in Mekeel's Weekly Stamp News, *July 4 and July 18, 1908. It is presented here because the tickets were issued for use all across America. H.N. Mudge provided us with an invaluable look at these tickets at a time when they were relatively fresh in his memory. Except for this single source of information, much of what is contained in "A Gleam of Light . . ." would be forever lost.*

The reader should also consult Richard Friedberg's "The Sleeping Car Mystery or Tracking the U.S. Revenue Stamped Paper X-Type Used on Railroad Tickets," published in the 1986 Congress Book. *Offprints are available from Mr. Friedberg, Masonic Building, Meadville, PA 16335.*